PRESENTED TO

FROM

ANGELS

TRUE STORIES

ROBERT J. MORGAN

THOMAS NELSON
Since 1798

NASHVILLE   DALLAS   MEXICO CITY   RIO DE JANEIRO

Angels
© 2011 by Robert J. Morgan

Published in Nashville, Tennessee, by Thomas Nelson. Thomas Nelson is a registered trademark of Thomas Nelson, Inc.

Cover and interior design by Koechel Peterson Design, Minneapolis, MN

Managing Editor: Lisa Stilwell

Thomas Nelson, Inc., titles may be purchased in bulk for educational, business, fund-raising, or sales promotional use. For information, please e-mail SpecialMarkets@ThomasNelson.com.

Italics in Scripture indicate the author's emphasis.

ISBN-13: 978-1-4041-8975-1

Printed in Singapore

12 13 14 15 [TWP] 6 5 4 3 2

To Ally

CONTENTS

INTRODUCTION | *All Night, All Day* 8

PART 1 | *Angels* 14

CHAPTER 1   What the Bible Says about Angels.......................16

CHAPTER 2   The Best Verse in the Bible about Angels...........26

CHAPTER 3   The Origin and Occupation of Angels 36

CHAPTER 4   The Power and Personality of Angels 46

CHAPTER 5   Angels in the Life of Christ 58

PART 2 | *Watching Over Me* 70

CHAPTER 6   Angels Transport Blessings to Our Lives............72

CHAPTER 7   Angels Deliver Us from Judgment.......................82

CHAPTER 8   Angels Protect Us in Danger 94

CHAPTER 9   Angels Assist God in Answering Our Prayers ...106

CHAPTER 10   Angels Teach Us to Worship...............................114

CHAPTER 11   Angels Usher Us to Heaven..................................126

CONCLUSION | *My Lord!* 136

NOTES | 140

ALL DAY,
all night

When my friend Richard Hendrix was ten years old, he lived in the small coal-mining town of Carbon Hill, Alabama. The Hendrix home sat on the edge of a forest and had a spanning porch where his mother and grandmother worked peeling apples or snapping beans. Richard loved to play with his friends in the nearby woods, especially around a large, overturned pine tree.

One day, as the family sat on the porch, a stranger approached. Since Carbon Hill was a small town, everyone knew the neighbors. The man, however, was unknown to them. He displayed Native American features and was toting a rifle. He asked if he could walk around and hunt snakes.

"Mama ordinarily would have told him to come back when Dad was home," Richard told me, "but for some reason she gave him permission. It seemed as though he belonged there; we felt safe in his presence."

The stranger walked straight down to the fallen pine tree as though he knew where he was going. It was a distance away, out of sight from the house, and no one had mentioned the spot to him. But, few moments later the air cracked with rifle shots. Shortly, the stranger reappeared with three large rattlesnakes. The largest had twenty rattlers. He had shot them where the children would soon have been playing. The man turned and walked back down the road and was never seen again.

"We asked about him," said Richard, "but nobody knew him, and nobody in the neighborhood saw him come or go. If any of us had been bitten by one of the snakes, we wouldn't have survived long enough to get to the hospital twenty miles away. I've always wondered if it was a coincidence or if we saw an angel without realizing it. I might not be alive today if not for this mysterious stranger showing up unannounced at our house that summer day in 1960."[1]

Coincidence? Mysterious stranger? Or angel? My files are bulging with stories like this, and many of them appear for the first time in print in this book. Some of these mysterious strangers are undoubtedly ordinary humans who showed up at just the right time in the providence of God. But I believe that others are angels, for the Bible speaks openly of their reality and activity in our world. Hebrews 13:2 says, "Do not forget to entertain strangers, for by so doing some people have entertained angels without knowing it."

This book represents a long-term effort on my part to understand the subject of angels in the teachings of the Bible and the story of Christ, in Christian and missionary history, and in everyday life. I'm not a speculator or enthusiast. I'm a Bible teacher devoted to "rightly dividing" the Word of God (2 Timothy 2:15 NKJV). There's no need

I believe that others are angels, for the Bible speaks openly of their reality and activity in our world.

to be fanciful or fanatical on this subject, for the Bible provides enough solid data for a satisfying understanding of these mysterious creatures. I'm not sure I've ever seen an angel, but I'm not sure I haven't. In these pages, I want to show you from Scripture and from a handful of first-person accounts what God's angels do—and what they do for us. As the hymnist said:

All night, all day.
Angels watching
over me,
my Lord.

I've seldom studied a topic that so uplifted my spirits. I hope this book will do the same for you. Many thanks to those who have helped in this effort, especially my editors, Jack Countryman, Laura Minchew, Lisa Stilwell, and Jennifer Barrow; my agent, Chris Ferebee; and my associates, Sherry Anderson, Joshua Rowe, Stephen Fox, Michael Walker, and David Gibson. These partners may not be angels, but they sure make an unbeatable team! I'm also eager to thank my wife, Katrina, for her support and advice. I'm grateful for all who have shared their "mysterious stranger" stories with me. If you have such a story, or you'd like more information about the resources we provide (including a study guide for this book), please contact me at www.robertjmorgan.com.

ALL NIGHT

PART ONE

Angels . . .

angels

ONE

WHAT THE BIBLE SAYS

about Angels

Dr. Richard Hipps, a friend from Memphis, shared something that happened to his grandmother in 1916. She was about ten, living with her widowed father in Asheville, North Carolina. He worked in the rock quarry. "Granny's job," said Richard, "was to take lunch to her father every day, but that required crossing a long bridge over the French Broad River. Granny was terrified of that bridge, and one day she was so overcome with fear that she couldn't bring herself to cross it. Sitting at the end of the bridge, she put her head down and began to cry. Suddenly she heard a voice saying, 'Honey, if you're afraid to cross the bridge, I'll walk with you.' Looking up, she saw a blue-eyed man with a bright countenance. He was holding his horse by the reins."

The horse and its rider escorted the little girl over the bridge, and all fear left her. They talked about the beauty of the blue sky and about the Lord's protective care. He told her she didn't need to be afraid anymore.

"As they approached the end of the bridge," Richard said, "Granny turned to thank the man for his company. Before her eyes, both he and his horse vanished."

Richard's grandmother continued telling this story into her eighties, and it served to comfort her throughout her life. Now it's a treasured story that has been passed down from generation to generation.[2]

This story sounds like so many of the Bible stories I've read since childhood. The Word of God is our primary source of information—the only authoritative and infallible one—on the intriguing subject of angels. It's easy to take flying leaps of fancy on this theme, but what does the Bible say?

That was my standard when I worked my way through every book of the Bible, tracking down each reference to angels until I came to the grand crescendo of angelic activity permeating the book of Revelation. I found 234 specific passages about angels, and another 278 times when God is

Angels are commonplace, a natural part of the environment.

referred to as the "Lord of hosts" ("hosts" being the angelic armies of heaven). Angels are referenced in thirty-nine books of the Bible—nineteen in the Old Testament and twenty in the New, and the range of angelic activity spans the Scriptures from Genesis 3:24 to Revelation 22:16. As John Hunter put it, "We can as easily think of summer without flowers as of the Bible without angels."[3]

As I pondered these passages, I was struck with how matter-of-factly the Bible treats this topic. The Lord doesn't try to convince us of the existence of angels or persuade us of their reality; He doesn't think of them as curious or bizarre creatures as we do, but as a normal part of His created order. In His world, angels are commonplace, a natural part of the environment. The biblical writers understood that there is a spiritual zone surrounding the earth where much unseen angelic and demonic activity exists. Famed pastor Charles Haddon Spurgeon once proclaimed, "I do not know how to explain it; I cannot tell how it is; but I believe angels have a great deal to do with the business of this world."[4]

In biblical text, angels pop in and out of stories as naturally as we'd drop into a coffee shop or duck out of an office. They're not mentioned gratuitously, and truth be told, it seems most Bible characters never knowingly saw an angel. Nevertheless, when needed, there they were. Angels comforted Hagar in the desert, delivered Lot from Sodom, guided Israel through the wilderness, fed Elijah under the juniper tree, surrounded Elisha with chariots of fire, saved Hezekiah from Assyria's onslaught, led Isaiah to spiritual commitment, directed Ezekiel into ministry, surrounded Jesus through every phase of His work, bore Lazarus to heaven, delivered Peter from prison, comforted Paul aboard a sinking ship, and gave John a VIP tour of New Jerusalem.

To believe the Bible is to believe in angels.

Sometimes these heavenly visitants appeared in human form and sometimes in superhuman splendor. Sometimes they were recognized as supernatural, but on other occasions they appeared as run-of-the-mill strangers. Sometimes the angels appeared in ones or twos, other times in multitudes. Some had wings; others didn't. Sometimes their feet were on the ground; sometimes they hovered in the sky. Often they materialized in three-dimensional reality, but occasionally they slipped into a person's dreams. Sometimes they were visible, but often they maintained their invisibility. In Revelation 18:1, an angel descended from heaven with such sunlike brilliance that the entire earth was illumined by his splendor.

I came away from my study realizing that when God made the cosmos, He created many diverse life forms—fungi and bacteria, plants and animals, fish and birds, humans and angels. To God, angels are just as conventional as any other creature; they're part of the diversity of life that fills heaven and earth. They are interplanetary creatures who travel easily and instantly between dimensions of reality, between the spiritual and physical realms. They are virtually everywhere, even around me as I write this book and around you as you read it. They comprise our celestial family.

As we trace this theme through the Bible, we find angels treated realistically, but not paraded or flaunted. Their existence and enterprises are assumed, and we're assured of their concern for us. But they are never hyperpresented in Scripture. In fact, as my friend Dr. David Jeremiah observed, "Everything Scripture says concerning angels is in connection with something else as the main theme. There are no pages or passages whose central purpose is to spell out a doctrine of angels."[5]

To me, this is an astounding insight that subtly demonstrates the truthfulness of Scripture. If I were composing a supernatural book like a Bible for the ages—if mere humans were putting it together—there would undoubtedly be effusive descriptions and details of these divine agents. But God's Word is written with an economy of words and a logical consistency of method. Nowhere do we find chunks of Scripture singularly devoted to angels. Every reference to angels in the Bible is incidental to a greater topic. Yet even with this observation, we don't lack for angelic material.

- Angels are active in Genesis, appearing in various forms at the gates of Eden, to Hagar, to Abraham, to Lot and the inhabitants of Sodom, and to Jacob. After Jacob, there's little mention of angels in the Pentateuch until we encounter the angel of the Lord, who accompanied Israel through the wilderness, and that "angel" was likely the preincarnate Christ Himself.[6]

- Judges has two prominent angel stories, and in subsequent books there are a few incidents involving angels in the careers of Saul, David, and Solomon. We also have another cluster of angelic sightings during the times of Elijah and Elisha.

- The Psalms give us a handful of precious verses about angels, though there are few references to angels in Proverbs or the other poetical books in the center of the Bible.

- Isaiah and Ezekiel had dramatic encounters with angels. The book of Daniel is full of angels, as is Zechariah. Few of the other Minor Prophets refer to angels.

- An explosion of angelic activity is connected with the ministry of Christ. Angels are involved in His birth, life, ministry, death, resurrection, ascension, and in the prophecies regarding His second coming.

- Angels occasionally showed up in the book of Acts with dramatic effect.

- There are sporadic references in the epistles to angels, giving us some intriguing hints and helps, yet no major passage in Paul's letters provides a systematic teaching about angels. We're given excellent information, however, in the book of Hebrews.

- The most intense concentration of angelic activity in the Bible is in the book of Revelation as it discloses their central role in heavenly worship, earthly tribulation, and in the victorious return and reign of Christ.

Of course, angelic activity didn't end with the book of Revelation, and the ministry of angels wasn't limited to the days of the Bible. Angels continue their nonstop work on behalf of the saints. Because we have biblical indications that demonic activity will increase as we draw closer to the end of the ages, it's only reasonable to assume the same of angelic enterprises.

When I was a student at Columbia International University, my next-door roommate was Terry Hammack, who, along with his wife, Sue, has faithfully served the Lord in Africa. Terry recently told me of his friend Janet Schneidermann, who labored more than forty years in northern Nigeria. She spent many of those years alone in the town of Gashua and was the only expatriate missionary within fifty miles. Much of her ministry was conducted against the backdrop of danger, and on one occasion she was warned by Nigerian colleagues to leave for a safer environment. Death threats were flying through the air like buzzards. Janet was a practitioner of Scripture memorization, and at the time she was committing Psalm 34:7 to heart: "The angel of the LORD encamps all around those who fear Him, and delivers them" (NKJV). As she meditated on that verse, she thought, *Thank You, Lord, for Your promise. Your protection is good enough for me, so I'm going to bed rather than leave my station.*

That night four men came from town to kill Janet. As they neared the secluded compound, they could see a tall man dressed in white with a sword in his hand guarding the front door. They were surprised and afraid because they had never seen a guard there before. They withdrew, and the next day they spied out the compound and questioned local informants. No one knew that Janet had hired a guard. That night the ruffians returned on the same mission. Again they were stopped dead in their tracks by this imposing guard.

The next day they casually "dropped by" to see Janet, feigning friendliness. In passing, they asked her about her guard. "I do not have a guard," she replied.

"We saw a huge man the last two nights with a long sword in his hand."

"Oh, him!" said Janet, laughing. "He must be the angel of the Lord that God promised to send because I fear Him." The men glanced at each other and hastily exited. No one ever approached her house again.[7]

The nineteenth-century Boston poet Lucy Larcom put it this way:

> *Blest were we,*
>
> *When every earthly prospect is shut in,*
>
> *And all our mortal helpers disappear,*
>
> *If, with Faith's eye undimmed and opened wide,*
>
> *We might behold the blessed angel-troop,*
>
> *Which God, our God, has promised shall encamp*
>
> *Round those who fear his name.*[8]

TWO

THE BEST VERSE
in the BIBLE
about Angels

Where the young man came from I don't know, and I never saw him again, but I've often wondered if he were an angel. I was returning from Africa with my twelve-year-old daughter, Grace, and after a stopover in Paris, we were in a rush to get to Charles de Gaulle Airport. As we sped out of the city, I wasn't sure we had boarded the right train. I nervously asked everyone within sight, "Is this the train to Charles de Gaulle?" With no English speakers in earshot, I gave up, pored over my maps, and hoped for the best.

Angelology is a therapeutic subject for our souls.

A few minutes later, the train stopped at an intermediate station and people began exiting. I glanced at my watch, worried about our tight connections and waiting for the doors to whoosh closed. Suddenly I heard a voice in perfect English: "If you're going to Charles de Gaulle Airport, you're on the wrong train." I looked up with surprise to find a young man sitting across from me. "The train you want," he said, "is there." He pointed to the other side of the platform.

With a quick "Thanks!" I leaped up and jerked Grace out the door. As we lugged our bags toward the other train, I heard his voice again. "Here!" He tossed me my backpack, which in my panic, I'd left on the seat. In it were our passports, plane tickets, identification, money, and credit cards.

Only after we collapsed on the airplane did I ponder what had happened. Where had the young man come from? Was it providential coincidence or an angelic visitation? I don't know, but I've had a nagging sense all these years that I may have encountered an angel unawares.

The Bible consistently affirms the existence of angels. They appear in its pages naturally, personally, and frequently. From Genesis to Revelation, the biblical writers weave angels in and out, and the teachings about angels are consistent and cohesive, rational, and logical.

Angelology is a therapeutic subject for our souls. The Lord must have wanted us to ponder the marvel of angels if He spoke of them so frequently. Colossians 3:2 tells us to set our minds on things above, not on things of earth. The "things above" certainly include the angelic world. Martin Luther said, "The acknowledgment of angels is needful in the church. Therefore godly preachers should teach them logically. . . . They should show what angels are. . . . They must speak touching their function. . . . In this sort ought we to teach with care, method, and attention, touching the sweet and loving angels."[9]

British historian Thomas B. Macaulay described the Puritans as people "whose minds had derived a peculiar advantage from the daily contemplation of superior beings and eternal interests."[10]

As I worked my way through the 234 passages in the Bible on this subject, one verse stood out in neon colors, providing a set of basic definitions for this strange species of creature. Hebrews 1:14 says, "Are not all angels ministering spirits sent to serve those who will inherit salvation?" In my opinion, this is the best verse about angels in the Bible.

You might want to put this book down and read the first chapter of Hebrews. You'll readily see the message that angels are subservient to Christ—made by and subject to Him.

When God the Son became human and took upon Himself the garb of flesh, He temporarily became a "little lower" than the angels He had created. Hebrews 2:9 says, "We see Jesus, who was made a little lower than the angels, now crowned with glory and honor because he suffered death."

Following His resurrection, Jesus resumed His full position and the prerogatives of His glory as He sat on heaven's throne, and the entire first chapter of Hebrews is devoted to telling us that He is as superior to the angels as the name He has inherited is superior to theirs (v. 4).

God the Father commands all the angels to worship Him (v. 6) and describes angels as "servants," while Jesus is referred to as "God" Himself, whose throne will last forever and ever (vv. 7–8). Which of the angels did God invite to sit at His right hand and rule with Him from the throne (v. 13)? None. Instead, "are not all angels ministering spirits sent to serve those who will inherit salvation?" (v. 14).

The idea of Hebrews 1, then, is that angels are created by and subject to Christ, who is both God and Lord. This is why angels hover worshipfully around the Lord Jesus in the biblical story, enveloping Him in His birth, during His ministry, and prophetically at His second coming. They gaze in awe at Him, and their example teaches us to love Him as well. They long to look into His work and redemption (1 Peter 1:12).

Hebrews 1:14 also describes the "physique" or substance of angels. They are "ministering spirits." This accounts for their invisibility, their ability to travel quickly, to fly between heaven and earth, to hover in the skies, to surround the throne in heaven one moment while transporting themselves to a needed spot on earth in the next. That's why they can bridge the chasm between the spiritual and physical realms in the blink of an eye.

What does the Bible mean by the phrase "ministering spirits"? This lies in the realm of mystery. Saint John of Damascus opined in the early 700s that angels were intelligent substances without matter or body. The delegates of the Second Council of Nicaea in AD 787 avowed that angels had bodies composed of light. The Council of the Lateran in AD 1215 decided they were incorporeal, having no bodies at all.[11] Martin Luther said in the early 1500s, "An angel is a spiritual creature created by God without a body for the service of Christendom."[12]

John Wesley suggested that angels are "not clogged with flesh and blood like us," but might have bodies of "a finer substance; resembling fire or flame."[13]

Nevertheless, at times they do appear in visible form, and we don't know if their bodies are material or immaterial, temporary or permanent, real or perceived. Theologian Charles Hodge suggested that there is nothing in the Bible that "proves that angels are absolutely destitute of proper material bodies of any kind."[14]

Whatever their construction and constitution, angels have a great purpose. They are *ministering* spirits sent to *serve* those who will inherit salvation. Notice the verb *sent*. If they are sent, there must be a Sender. They are God's response to our needs. He sends them to aid those who inherit salvation.

Dr. Albert Barnes observed:

Angels are sent to be [our] attendants. . . . Kings and princes are surrounded by armed men, or by sages called to be their counsellors; but the most humble saint may be encompassed by a retinue of beings of far greater power, and more elevated rank. . . . [Angels] come to attend the redeemed; they wait on their steps; they sustain them in trial; they accompany them when departing to heaven. It is a higher honor to be attended by one of those pure intelligences, than by the most elevated monarch that ever swayed a sceptre, or wore a crown.[15]

Exactly how do angels serve those who inherit salvation? The Bible gives us some clues, but many Christians can also speak from experience.

My friend Dr. Mary Ruth Wisehart told me of a time she was traveling alone to Spain. She's an independent traveler with a can-do attitude, but on this trip she was tired and unable to manage stairs. She was the last passenger to disembark from her overnight flight. Clutching two bags, she started through the labyrinth of passageways toward passport control. When she encountered a marble stairway with no handrails, she paused and told herself, "I guess I can make this." But as she stood at the top of the steps trying to visualize her descent, she heard a voice behind her speaking with an accent she couldn't detect. "Don't worry," he said. "I will help you." The young man had a backpack, and Dr. Wisehart couldn't see his face very well under his cap. Taking her bags, he helped her down the steps, then quickly disappeared ahead of her, running toward baggage claim.

An angel is a spiritual creature created by God without a body for the service of Christendom.

Dr. Wisehart soon came to another stairway. She said to herself, "Well, I guess I can make this somehow." Suddenly the same voice spoke from behind. "Don't worry, I will help you." Taking her bags, he helped her down the steps; then he again ran ahead and disappeared before my friend could thank him.

"I don't know whether he was an angel," Dr. Wisehart told me, "but I think God sent him."[16]

John Wesley once preached a sermon about angels, saying that they minister to us "in a thousand ways which we do not now understand. They may prevent our falling into many dangers, which we are not sensible of; and may deliver us out of many others, though we know not whence our deliverance comes. How many times have we been strangely and accountably preserved . . . ! And it is well if we did not impute that preservation to chance, or to our own wisdom or strength. Not so: it was God (who) gave His angels charge over us, and in their hands they bore us up."[17]

For after all, are not all angels ministering spirits sent to serve those who will inherit salvation?

The book of Hebrews
begins and ends with twin verses
about angels.

Angels

HEBREWS 1:14 TELLS US WHAT ANGELS DO FOR US.

*They are ministering spirits sent
to serve those who inherit salvation.*

HEBREWS 13:2 TELLS US WHAT WE DO FOR ANGELS.

*In showing hospitality to strangers
we could be entertaining them unaware.*

THREE

THE ORIGIN *and* OCCUPATION

of Angels

36

As Merle and Gloria Inniger traveled from Pakistan to America, they stopped in London for a few days, and somewhere along the way Merle managed to lock the doors of the rental car and lose the keys. It was Saturday afternoon, and no locksmiths answered the phone. The rental car company said they didn't have a spare key.

Merle and Gloria panicked about missing their flight home. Two Christian friends came to commiserate, and the four bowed their heads and prayed for help. As they finished, they looked up as a strange man approached. He offered his keys to them. The man explained he owned a similar car and perhaps his keys would work.

Merle inserted the key into the door, but it was no match. On a lark, he walked around to the trunk. To his amazement, the key fit perfectly and the lid popped open. There on the floor of the trunk were his keys. They had apparently fallen earlier while he was taking something out. "Praise the Lord!" everyone shouted as Merle grabbed the keys. But when he turned to thank the stranger, no one was in sight. They looked in all directions, but the man had vanished. Later, Merle asked a locksmith about the chance of the man's key fitting his trunk. It was about one in twenty thousand.

"An angel?" Merle later wondered. "I have always felt he must have been."[18]

We mustn't think of angels yet as genies or errand boys who fly to our aid at every daily dilemma. The Bible provides a balanced perspective, and it's helpful to look at angels as Scripture does. What does the Bible say about the origin and occupation of angels?

ANGELS APPEAR EARLY IN THE BIBLE.

Both the Old and New Testaments begin with angelic appearances right off the bat. The first angel in Scripture appeared in Genesis 3, guarding the path to the Tree of Life. In the Gospels, we encounter an angel before finishing the first chapter of the first Gospel—an angel appeared to Joseph in a dream, advising him to take Mary as his wife (Matthew 1:20).

ANGELS WERE PRESENT WHEN GOD CREATED THE UNIVERSE.
Since they're created beings, they're not eternal in the sense that God is infinite. They were created by Him. But the Bible doesn't tell us exactly *when* they were made. Job 38:7 implies that angels were present at the creation of the universe, and Ezekiel 28:13–14 and Genesis 3:24 tell us angels were on hand in the garden of Eden. It seems that angels were among the first on God's agenda of creation.

ANGELS EXIST TO DO GOD'S BIDDING.
Perhaps the best Old Testament verses about angels are Psalm 103:20–21: "Praise the Lord, you his angels, you mighty ones who do his bidding, who obey his word. Praise the Lord, all his heavenly hosts, you his servants who do his will." Notice the fourfold way angels are described: *His angels*, *mighty ones*, *heavenly hosts*, and *His servants*. Notice their threefold commitment to fulfill *His bidding*, *His word*, and *His will*. And don't miss the beginning of the verse: they are commanded to actively praise Him, to bless the Lord.

ANGELS TRAVEL SWIFTLY BETWEEN HEAVEN AND EARTH.

One of the most fascinating Bible texts about angels occurs when the patriarch Jacob stops to rest in Genesis 28. He was trekking through the desert when the sun descended behind the western dunes, and he found a stone to use as a pillow. That night, Jacob dreamed of an immense staircase from heaven to earth. The angels of God were traveling back and forth, ascending and descending. As hymnist Fanny Crosby put it, "Angels descending bring from above echoes of mercy, whispers of love."

When he woke from his dream, Jacob was overwhelmed. "Surely the LORD is in this place," he said, "and I was not aware of it. . . . How awesome is this place! This is none other than the house of God; this is the gate of heaven" (vv. 16–17). Science fiction writers often speak of a wormhole—a theoretical passageway or shortcut—in space. I don't know about wormholes, but Genesis 28 teaches that there are gateways between heaven and earth, and angels are constantly coming and going.

Angels descending bring from above echoes of mercy, whispers of love.

As we visualize the scene, we're prone to see it in slow motion, angels gracefully gliding up and down the stairs like hot air balloons rising and descending. But angels can also move quickly. In Daniel 9:21, the angel Gabriel was sent from heaven with a message, and he came "in swift flight."

How astounding to realize that we constantly live on holy ground, in the presence of the Lord and His angels. Look around right now. You can repeat Jacob's words as your own: "Surely the Lord is in the place, and I did not realize it. How awesome!" Whether you're reading this in your living room, at your bedside, on an airplane, or in a hospital or jail, you're on holy ground if Christ is your Lord and Savior. That leads to my next observation . . .

ANGELS CONSTANTLY PATROL THE EARTH.

When I began pastoring shortly after my college years, I chose the book of Zechariah as one of my first pulpit projects. In retrospect, it wasn't very smart. Zechariah is a mysterious book with a dizzying array of images, visions, and prophecies—not a good choice for a novice pastor. But I was drawn to the book, and I still am. Zechariah cracks the door into spiritual realms and lets us feel some of the invisible hum in the unseen dimensions around us.

In the opening chapters, Zechariah had a series of visions in a single night. In the first one, he saw an assortment of horses and horsemen among the myrtle trees near Jerusalem. When he asked about them, he was told, "They are the ones the LORD has sent out to patrol the earth. . . ." As Zechariah listened, the riders reported to their superior, "We have been patrolling the earth, and the whole earth is at peace" (1:10–11 NLT).

These were evidently God's Special Forces, an invisible team of angels who had been circling the earth observing the political and military activities of the nations. They were reporting to someone of higher rank.

Since this is a vision, we don't have to take everything literally. Angels certainly patrol the earth, but do they actually ride horses? I don't know. It's not impossible, of course. If the Lord made earthly horses, He can certainly create angelic ones. (Remember the story at the beginning of chapter one!) Whether or not the horses are literal or figurative, the point is the same: angels are constantly monitoring the activities of "earthlings" like us.

ANGELS ARE OFTEN DESCRIBED IN MILITARY TERMS.
They are called a "host," or army. The apostle John, in his vision of the second coming of Christ, wrote, "The armies of heaven were following him" (Revelation 19:14). The prophet Micaiah said, "I saw the LORD sitting on his throne with all the host of heaven standing around him on his right and on his left" (1 Kings 22:19). In Joshua 5:15, an imposing military general—apparently superhuman—appeared to Joshua on the outskirts of

Jericho and identified himself as the "commander of the LORD's army."

In the Gospels, Jesus avowed He could have called more than twelve legions of angels had He chosen. *Legion* was a military term for a division of several thousand soldiers.

Angels are often seen with swords in their hands, such as the cherub barring the way to the Tree of Life in Genesis 3, the angel blocking Balaam's way in Numbers 22, and the angel suspended over Jerusalem in 1 Chronicles 21.

In Daniel and Revelation, we're told of great wars and spiritual conflicts being fought in invisible realms. Ephesians 1:21 says that Jesus Christ is enthroned "far above all principality and power and might and dominion" (NKJV). Later, we read these astonishing words: "For we do not wrestle against flesh and blood, but against principalities, against powers, against the rulers of the darkness of this age, against spiritual hosts of wickedness in the heavenly places" (6:12 NKJV).

The demonic forces around us are more pervasive and persuasive than we know, but those *for* us are greater than those *against* us. A powerful throng of angels keeps an unseen vigil, and we can say with Luther: "And though this world, with devils filled, should threaten to undo us, we will not fear, for God hath willed His truth to triumph through us."[19]

In 2 Kings 6, the prophet Elisha incurred the fury of the king of Syria, who sent forces to capture him. One night while Elisha was sleeping in the town of Dothan, the Syrian army silently surrounded and sealed off the city. In the morning, Elisha's servant rose, saw they were trapped, and ran to the prophet crying, "Alas, my master! What shall we do?" (v. 15 NKJV)

The prophet was nonplussed. "Don't be afraid," he said. "Those who are with us are more than those who are with them." Elisha offered a simple prayer: "Lord, open his eyes so he may see." For a passing moment, the servant received enhanced eyesight that allowed him to view the unseen realm. "He looked and saw the hills full of horses and chariots of fire all around Elisha" (vv. 16–17).

Whatever our situation, we have an invisible army of powerful agents surrounding us and guarding us. We can say with the writer of Psalm 27: "The Lord is my light and my salvation; whom shall I fear? The Lord is the strength of my life; of whom shall I be afraid? . . . Though an army may encamp against me, my heart shall not fear" (vv. 1, 3 NKJV).

We aren't fitted with special-vision goggles allowing us to see the army of angels patrolling the world or surrounding the saints. Our human ears cannot hear the trumpet blasts, the clashing of swords, or the thundering of the troops. But the Bible leaves no doubt: "The angel of the Lord encamps all around those who fear Him, and delivers them" (Psalm 34:7 NKJV).

As Charles Wesley put it:

WHICH OF THE MONARCHS OF THE EARTH

Can boast a guard like ours,

ENCIRCLED FROM OUR SECOND BIRTH

With all the heavenly powers?

MYRIADS OF BRIGHT, CHERUBIC BANDS,

Sent by the King of kings,

REJOICE TO BEAR US IN THEIR HANDS,

And shade us with their wings.

FOUR

THE POWER
and
PERSONALITY

of Angels

Sharnel Smith and her husband, Rick, were educators in Nigeria, stationed at a Bible college in a remote region. They had no electricity except their generator and no running water except what they pumped.

One day, Sharnel decided to leave her rural campus and drive to the city of Billiri for market day. Their old Peugeot 304 pickup truck had to be pushed off and kick-started. She asked six of her students to ride in the back. In exchange for taking them to the market, they agreed to push the truck off so everyone could get home again.

It was a clear day, blazing hot. Sharnel got all her shopping done, and everyone loaded their purchases into the back of the truck. The students pushed the truck out of the dirt parking lot and were getting ready to give it a heave-ho when Sharnel slammed the brakes. A group of about thirty children was gathering around the truck and parted to let a ten-year-old boy approach. Sharnel's window was down, and she saw he was beating a drum, something black wrapped around his neck. He reminded Sharnel of a pied piper. The black scarf around his neck, she realized, was a black snake.

Growing up in the rural U.S., it wasn't uncommon for Sharnel's friends to have pet snakes. "Seeing a boy with his pet snake wasn't scary at all. I thought, *Ah, a kid with a pet snake. No wonder the other children are following him*."

The boy greeted her with a big smile and asked if she'd like to see his snake. "Sure," she said. She took the four-foot snake as he handed it to her headfirst. She grabbed its neck with her right hand, gripped the rest of it with her left hand. The snake tried to turn its head to Sharnel and hiss, but at that point, she "literally sensed the wing of an angel between that snake and me, and I remember looking at that snake in the eyes and saying to it, 'Now just hush.'"

She turned and handed the snake back to the boy. Suddenly the six Bible college students were around her, faces aghast. "Ma, do you know what you just did?" About a hundred people had congregated around the truck.

"No, what's going on? I just held that boy's pet snake."

"Ma, that is the witch doctor's son. You just held a spitting cobra, and it did not bite or strike you. All these people are saying you know how to charm snakes since it didn't harm you."

"But it was just a little boy with a pet snake!"

"No, Ma. The witch doctors casts spells over snakes so they won't harm their children, but to all others there is no protection. They do this to prove how much power they have."

Suddenly Sharnel realized why God sent an angel to spread its protecting wing as a barrier between her and the cobra. Otherwise, "I would have traveled home in a pine box." That day the village of Billiri saw dramatic evidence of the authority of Christ and that an angel's wing is stronger than a serpent's hiss.[20]

ANGELS HAVE PARANORMAL POWERS.

Angels provide help and protection in times of need.

In studying angels in the Bible, it's obvious that God's secret agents are glorious beings of superhuman strength and supernatural abilities. Adam and Eve were arguably the two best specimens of physicality in history, uniquely designed and personally built by God Himself. But in Genesis 3, they instinctively realized they were no match for the cherub with the flaming sword who blocked the way to the Tree of Life. The first couple didn't try to challenge this shining being.

In 2 Kings 19:35, a solitary angel wiped out the entire Assyrian army. It was the strangest battle in military history, and it changed the course of world events. Isaiah 37:36 says, "Then the angel of the LORD went out and put to death a hundred and eighty-five thousand men in the Assyrian camp. When the people got up the next morning—there were all the dead bodies!"

It was an angel who rolled back the massive stone at the tomb of Christ as though it were made of Styrofoam. Additionally, the book of Revelation gives us one account after another of cataclysmic events unleashed on the earth by powerful angels in waves of judicial wrath and divine justice.

Angels are not omnipotent or almighty, as God is. There are limitations to their strength. But they are "muscular" beings, and they operate with the full authority of God as they do His bidding. They are powerful in dispensing judgment, but they're also strong on our behalf as they provide help and protection in times of need.

ANGELS HAVE THE POWER TO OBSERVE OUR LIVES.

Among their superhuman powers is the ability to watch us without our realizing it. The apostle Paul said that he and his fellow apostles were constantly on display "to the whole universe, to angels as well as to men" (1 Corinthians 4:9). When Paul instructed Timothy about the ministry, he said he was doing so in the presence of the holy angels (1 Timothy 5:21). Paul warned us to worship in appropriate ways at church "because of the angels" (1 Corinthians 11:10). Angels were watching over Hagar in the desert, for example, and monitoring Peter's condition in prison in Acts 12 and Paul's on a sinking ship in Acts 27. No detail escaped their eye.

A writer from yesteryear suggested that many secret sins would be restrained if we simply remembered a fourfold reality: "When we are alone—it would keep us from many sins . . . [to realize that] God seeth, and conscience within seeth, and angels without are witnesses; they grieve at it, and the devils about us rejoice at it."[21] In other words, God is always observing us, our conscience is aware of what we do in secret, and we are in full view of both angels (who are grieved when we sin) and demons (who rejoice when we fall).

ANGELIC STRENGTH IS MULTIPLIED BY THEIR NUMBERS.
There is strength in numbers, and the Bible tells us that the angelic population is virtually innumerable. Job asks, "Can his forces be numbered?" (25:3). I've already mentioned that Jesus had access to at least twelve legions of angels, "legion" being a division of several thousand men. He could have summoned a hundred thousand angels without even snapping His fingers.

The Bible alludes to different orders and ranks of angels, highly organized and managed, like a mighty military machine armed for the ages. Notice the interesting phraseology of Psalm 68:17: "The chariots of God are tens of thousands and thousands of thousands." Here the word *chariots* seems to be a synonym for "angels," and "tens of thousands and thousands of thousands" is a Hebrew expression for "innumerable."

When the prophet Daniel was allowed a glimpse of heaven's throne, he saw it surrounded by "ten thousand times ten thousand" (7:10). The writer of Hebrews spoke of "thousands upon thousands of angels in joyful assembly" (12:22).

At the birth of Christ, "a great company of the heavenly host" appeared in the night skies over Bethlehem (Luke 2:13).

In Revelation 9:16, John describes a swarm of demons ascending like locusts from the abyss during the tribulation of the last days. He said, "The number of the mounted troops was two hundred million." If that represents only a portion of the population of fallen angels—and if fallen angels are only a third of all the angels God created (see Revelation 12:4)—then the number of good angels must be incalculable.

That brings up another curious fact. In the Bible, we're given the names of only two good angels—Gabriel and Michael. That every angel has both name and personality is without question. When we read the angel stories of the Bible, we can easily see humor in some, anger in others, compassion and concern in most of the stories. When they worship, it's with exuberance. When they battle, it is with determination. It seems that angels have emotions not unlike those we experience. Jesus told us they rejoice when one soul on earth confesses Him as Lord (Luke 15:10).

So angels have intellect, emotions, and volition. They are "persons" just as we are persons and as each member of the Godhead is a person. One day, we'll have a long list of angelic names in our contact lists, but for now we're told the names of only Gabriel and Michael.

Gabriel is the angel of the annunciation. In Daniel 8 and 9, he imparts messianic information to Daniel. In Luke, this same character pays a visit to Zechariah and to Mary, announcing the births of John and Jesus respectively. His duty in Scripture was to prophetically preannounce the coming of the Messiah.

Michael, on the other hand, appears in a more militant role. He is called an archangel, and we meet him in the books of Daniel, Jude, and Revelation. He seems to be the guardian angel of Israel, who engages in battle in the spiritual realms on behalf of God's chosen people.

ANGELS ARE FELLOW SERVANTS WITH US.

As I read the "angel verses," two jumped off the page like living letters and took me by surprise. In Revelation 19:10, John was so overwhelmed by his vision that he fell down to worship the angel. The angel quickly said, "Do not do it! I am a fellow servant with you and with your brothers who hold to the testimony of Jesus. Worship God!" Three chapters later, John repeated his mistake (22:8–9).

Here is the Bible's most startling description of angels. They are *fellow servants* with us. The Greek term is *sundoulos*. The prefix *sun* means "with," and *doulos* means a "servant." In eternity—on the new earth and in the new heavens and in the celestial city of New Jerusalem—we'll be fellow workers and next-door neighbors with angels. We'll be serving the same cause and worshipping the same triune God. Nineteenth-century Scottish preacher Norman Macleod suggested that we'll discover on reaching heaven that God's angels are not strangers but old friends who have known all about us from the day of our birth till the hour of our death.[22]

For now, it's enough to know that our angelic "fellow workers" have the power to help us in ways suited to our circumstances—even if it means kicking us in the ribs.

One of my favorite angel stories in the Bible is in Acts 12. Simon Peter had been arrested by King Herod, who intended to execute him. He was bound by two chains in the Roman prison, and guarded by sixteen highly disciplined Imperial soldiers. Sentries stood outside the cell. No Houdini on earth could have escaped.

Peter fully expected to lose his life, but that didn't keep him from falling into a deep sleep between two of his guards. The apostle's simple faith in Christ was a better comforter than the softest mattress or warmest blanket. During the night, God sent an angel to break Peter out of jail. It's hard not to smile when you read verses 7–19: "Suddenly an angel of the Lord appeared and a light shone in the cell. He struck Peter on the side and woke him up. 'Quick, get up!' he said, and the chains fell off Peter's wrists."

The angel told Peter to hurry and dress. Peter did so but thought he was dreaming or having a vision. "They passed the first and second guards and came to the iron gate leading to the city. It opened for them by itself, and they went through it. When they had walked the length of one street, suddenly the angel left him." Peter came to himself and said, "Now I know without a doubt that the Lord sent His angel and rescued me from Herod's clutches."

Meanwhile there was "no small commotion" among the soldiers as to what had become of Peter. Herod searched the prison top to bottom, then cross-examined the hapless guards and had them executed. Later, in his headquarters in Caesarea, while he was sitting on his throne and congratulating himself, another angel (or maybe the same one) showed up unseen by human eyes. Acts 12:23 says, "Because Herod did not give praise to God, an angel of the Lord struck him down, and he was eaten by worms and died."

Acts 12, then, contains two angel stories: an apostle rescued from execution and a tyrant put to death. It pays to be on the right side of things!

The same angels at work in Acts 12 are still doing God's bidding. They are both our fellow servants and powerful spirits sent to serve those who inherit salvation. Phillips Brooks, the famous Boston pastor and the author of "O Little Town of Bethlehem," said, "I am sure that God and His angels help many a struggler who does not know where the help comes from."[23]

Sometimes that struggler is you or me.

FIVE

Angels

in the LIFE of CHRIST

*P*eter Marshall was a Scottish-American preacher who served as chaplain of the United States Senate until suffering a fatal heart attack at a relatively young age in 1949. His wife, Catherine, later wrote a biography of him that became one of the best-loved books of the twentieth century. In *A Man Called Peter*, Catherine recounts an incident that happened when Peter was a young fellow working in the English village of Bamburgh, not far from the Scottish border. To the west were the desolate heights of Chalton Moor, an area known for its limestone:

> Walking back from a nearby village to Bamburgh one dark, starless night, Peter struck out across the moors, thinking he would take a shortcut. He knew there was a deserted limestone quarry close by Glororum Road, but he thought

he could avoid the danger spot. The night was inky black, eerie. There was only the sound of the wind through the heather-strained moorland, the noisy clamor of a wild muir fowl as his footsteps disturbed them, the occasional far-off bleating of a sheep.

Suddenly he heard someone call, *"Peter!..."* There was great urgency in the voice.

He stopped. "Yes, who is it? What do you want?"

For a second he listened, but there was no response, only the sound of the wind. The moor seemed completely deserted.

Thinking he must have been mistaken, he walked on a few paces. Then he heard it again, even more urgently:

"Peter!"

He stopped dead still, trying to peer into that impenetrable darkness, but suddenly stumbled and fell to his knees. Putting out his hand to catch himself, he found nothing there. As he cautiously investigated, feeling around in a semicircle, he found himself to be on the very brink of an abandoned stone quarry. Just one more step would have sent him plummeting into space to certain death.[24]

If a man called Peter heard an angel's voice and received angelic protection, what can we say about a man named Jesus? If angels are sent to serve those who inherit salvation, how much greater is their desire to serve Him who provided salvation? If we have a few angelic experiences clustered around the stories of Abraham, Moses, and Elijah, what should we expect when Jesus Christ appeared in the towns and byways of Israel?

Just as our Lord's ministry seemed to trigger an uptick in demonic activity, we also see a concentration of angelic activity centered around His earthly life. Paul said angels were constant onlookers during His ministry: "He appeared in a body, was vindicated by the Spirit, was seen by angels" (1 Timothy 3:16).

Angels are prominent players in seven great epochs in the story of Christ.

First, His birth. There are six known sightings of angels connected with our Lord's nativity. The first was Gabriel's visit to Zechariah in Luke 1, telling him that he and his aged wife would conceive and bear the forerunner for Christ. Then Gabriel trekked to Nazareth to tell Mary she would be "overshadowed" by the Holy Spirit and would give birth to the Messiah. The angel appeared three times to Joseph in dreams, advising him every step of the way. We also have the spectacular scene over the fields of Bethlehem as the sky erupted in the greatest choir of angels in history, at least until Christ returns.[25]

We next encounter angels at the beginning of Jesus' ministry, at His temptation in the wilderness. Following His tug-of-war with Satan, "the devil left him, and angels came and attended him" (Matthew 4:11). In those days, He "was with the wild animals, and angels attended him" (Mark 1:13).

The third time we encounter angels in the life of Christ is within His teaching, for He revealed previously classified information about them during His sermons. He explained that angels are genderless by nature. They neither marry nor are given in marriage, nor do they die (Matthew 22:30; Luke 20:36). He also told us they're not omniscient. There are some things they don't know, such as the timing of His return (Mark 13:32). Jesus told us that angels rejoice when people are saved (Luke 15:10) and that angels are travel guides, so to speak. They escort believers into heaven at the time of death (16:22).

Jesus also made this astonishing claim in John 1:51: "I tell you the truth, you shall see heaven open, and the angels of God ascending and descending on the Son of Man." He was comparing Himself to Jacob's ladder in Genesis 28. Jacob dreamed of a staircase stretching from earth to heaven, and he called the place Bethel, which means the "Gate of God." Jesus was saying, in effect, "Jacob's ladder was a prototype or preview of Me. I am the connecting link between heaven and earth. As the God-man, I am the real Bethel, and I'm compassed by angels who come and go at My command."

We've already seen that Jesus could summon legions of angels at any moment, should He choose. Our Lord never gave a sermon on angelology, but as He spoke on other subjects, He mentioned angels. He always did so as though He possessed full knowledge of them and exercised full authority over the unseen realms.

Fourth, we have a plaintive glimpse of angelic activity on the night He was betrayed. Jesus prayed so earnestly on that evening that His sweat was like drops of blood. But Luke 22:43 tells us, "An angel from heaven appeared to him and strengthened him."

That strange and wonderful verse reminds me of a story in *The Ecclesiastical History of Socrates Scholasticus*, an early book of church history that documents the time from Emperor Constantine to the days of Theodosius II, a period of 140 years. It was written by Socrates of Constantinople, who was born in the fourth century. In his history of the church in Roman times, Socrates tells of a young man named Theodore who was subjected to cruel torture under the direction of Emperor Julian the Apostate. The young man was later

An angel from heaven appeared to him and strengthened him.

asked about the pain he endured. Which was worse—the scourging or the rack? Theodore replied he was not able to answer that question, because during the torture a young man suddenly appeared beside him and, using a soft and cooling linen, wiped away the sweat, cooled him with water, and so strengthened his mind that the time of trial became a season of rapture rather than of suffering.[26]

Similarly, in the Garden of Gethsemane, an angel appeared to our Lord and strengthened Him. Yet with that one exception, there is a total silence regarding angelic activity at Calvary. Though He could have summoned all the legions of heaven, He died alone. It appears that for six hours one Friday the angels were told to stand down. We can only imagine their perplexity as they watched from afar.

But when Easter Sunday dawned, the angels sprang into action again— for the fifth time. All four Gospels describe the role of angels that day. Matthew 28 tells us that as the women arrived at the tomb of Jesus, "There was a violent earthquake, for an angel of the Lord came down from heaven and, going to the tomb, rolled back the stone and sat on it. His appearance was like lightning, and his clothes were white as snow. The guards were so afraid of him that they shook and became like dead men" (vv. 2–4).

As the women entered the tomb, they didn't find it empty at all. "They saw a young man dressed in a white robe sitting on the right side, and they were alarmed. 'Don't be alarmed,' he said. 'You are looking for Jesus the Nazarene, who was crucified. He has risen!'" (Mark 16:5–6).

Luke adds that the Easter angels appeared to be two men arrayed in a startling wardrobe—"in clothes that gleamed like lightning" (24:4). Mary Magdalene saw "two angels in white, seated where Jesus' body had been, one at the head and the other at the foot. They asked her, 'Woman, why are you crying?'" (John 20:12–13).

Each of the Gospel writers tells the story from his own singular perspective. There's no evidence of collusion, no attempt to get their story together. The differences in the details are not contradictions, just distinctions of perspective. The accounts smack of authenticity, as each author wants us to know one thing above all else—Jesus rose from the dead.

The sixth time we see angels around the life of Christ is at His ascension. According to Acts 1:9, Jesus was taken up before their eyes, and a cloud hid Him from their sight. The next two verses say: "They were looking intently up into the sky as he was going, when suddenly two men dressed in white stood beside them. 'Men of Galilee,' they said, 'why do you stand here looking into the sky? This same Jesus . . . will come back'" (vv. 10–11).

That brings us to the seventh epoch of angels in the life of Christ—at His return. Jesus will come in His Father's glory with His angels (Matthew 16:27). He said He would come in the clouds of the sky with power and great glory and with His angels (24:30–31). The apostle Paul declared that when the Lord Himself comes from heaven, it will be with a shout, "with the voice of the archangel and with the trumpet call of God" (1 Thessalonians 4:16). He will be "revealed from heaven in blazing fire with his powerful angels" (2 Thessalonians 1:7).

There's also the book of Revelation, where the word *angel* occurs more than eighty times. The angels mobilize during every phase of the events of the last days, and they will accompany our Lord's return to earth with shouts and songs and power and dominion. At the moment of His return, the choirs of heaven will burst into a Hallelujah Chorus that will reverberate through the entire universe: "Hallelujah! For our Lord God Almighty reigns. Let us rejoice and be glad and give him glory! For the wedding of the Lamb has come . . ." (19:6–7).

Angels have worshiped and adored God the Son since the day He created them. They praised Christ before His birth in Bethlehem and then watched in wonderment as He descended to our planet. They hovered around Him during His earthly ministry, were silent as He died for the world, and erupted in joy as they announced His resurrection. They provided the commentary for His return to heaven and took their place as He resumed His reign on the throne of glory, far above all rule and authority and power and dominion. Peter said that Jesus is at God's right hand, with angels, authorities, and powers in submission to Him. The book of Hebrews says, "Let all God's angels worship Him" (1:6). And at this moment, they are straining in excitement as He prepares for His second coming.

Do you realize that we ourselves often encourage the angels to praise Him? How could we—sinful earthlings—have the audacity to command the angels to worship our Lord and theirs? Yet that's what we do every time we sing the doxology at church. By our songs, we encourage the heavenly host to join us as we worship Him in exuberant praise.

Praise God from whom all blessings flow;

Praise Him all creatures here below;

Praise Him above, ye heav'nly host;

Praise Father, Son, and Holy Ghost.

Amen!

Angels

HAVE WORSHIPED AND

ADORED GOD THE SON

since the day He created them.

PART TWO

Watching Over Me

SIX

Angels

TRANSPORT BLESSINGS *to* OUR LIVES

The word *horrific* comes to mind whenever I read of Idi Amin's reign of terror in Uganda in the 1970s. Charles Okwir lived through that period, and he credits God's angels with caring for him at certain key moments, especially in 1973. That year, Charles saw people around him mercilessly killed, and he himself was chosen for death several times. But each attempt on his life was mysteriously thwarted.

"One evening I had gone to buy essential goods from town," he said. "On my way home I met Amin's soldiers, who had mounted a roadblock, and people were being knifed. Many were forced to lie on the ground, and I watched as they were as bludgeoned to death. Blood was everywhere. But the angel of the Lord blindfolded the eyes of the soldiers as I rode past on my bicycle. The soldiers did not see me. I passed by completely unnoticed, as if invisible.

"Another evening as I rode past a dangerous area, a soldier in full uniform jumped out from the bush, his gun cocked and pointing at me. But he was trembling. He cried, 'What's wrong with you? I wanted to kill you, but I cannot. What is your secret? Where have you been and where are you going?'"

Charles told him he'd been doing God's work and was returning home. The soldier backed away, hand shaking. "Your God is great," he exclaimed. "Go and pray for me too." Charles went on his way, amazed at whatever unseen force had saved his life.

On another day—a Sunday—Charles was arrested and driven into the bush to be killed. A soldier with a loaded pistol ordered him out of the vehicle. "Say whatever you want to say before I kill you," barked the soldier. Charles thanked him for the opportunity and calmly explained his message and his mission for Christ. "If you kill me," he concluded, "you are sending me Home." Inexplicably, Charles was released.

Charles was mysteriously protected more times than he can recount. Sometimes, he said, he was warned in a dream to leave a particular area before the killers arrived. Other times he learned that soldiers sent to arrest him had broken down on the road. "These are just a few of the instances of the Lord and His angels protecting me," said Charles Okwir, who is still faithfully serving the Lord today as a pastor in Lira, Uganda.[27]

My friend Dr. Homer Coker has a far different story. The threat on his life came from heart disease. He was a professor and researcher at Georgia State University. One night in 2004 he awoke with pains in his chest. He knew it was a heart attack. He opened his eyes and saw a man standing at the foot of his bed.

"Homer, I'm your guardian angel," the man said. "I've come to take you home."

Homer felt peace and said simply, "Okay."

The man disappeared, and Homer lay there trying to make sense of it. A moment later the man reappeared, smiled at him, waved, and disappeared again. Homer went on to the hospital, where doctors confirmed he had indeed suffered a heart attack. But he recovered with a feeling that for some reason he'd been granted an extension of time on earth. "To this day," he said, "I believe very strongly that this guy was real—an angel."[28]

We seldom see our encamping angels, but they are on duty around the clock. Consider the curious reference to angels in Genesis 32. Jacob had decided to return home from a prolonged stay in Mesopotamia. Years before, as a young scoundrel, he had fled, having deceived his father and conned his brother Esau. Esau had sworn to kill him, and as far as Jacob knew, Esau, now a mighty sheik, still wanted him dead. Nevertheless, as God worked in his heart, Jacob knew he had to go home.

That's when we come to a cryptic passage: "Jacob also went on his way, and the angels of God met him. When Jacob saw them, he said, 'This is the camp of God!' So he named the place Mahanaim" (vv. 1–2). That's the entire passage; there is no further explanation. But we do know that *Mahanaim* means "two camps."

Jacob was traveling with his family and a few servants, and they set up camp in the desert for the night. Apparently a band of angelic troopers was traveling alongside them unseen, and they too stopped there for the night. For a few moments, Jacob was allowed to see the contingent of angels encamped around him. How it must have encouraged Jacob to realize that God's angels were protecting him, conveying God's grace into his heart.

The "two camp" experience doesn't belong just to Jacob. It's for all God's children. Psalm 34:7 says, "The angel of the LORD encamps around those who fear him, and he delivers them."

In the Bible, angels even provided physical necessities like food and water for God's people. When Hagar and her son were parched in the desert, an angel opened her eyes to see a nearby well (Genesis 21:19). When Elijah had a nervous breakdown, the angel of the Lord found him sleeping under a juniper tree in the desert. "All at once an angel touched him and said, 'Get up and eat.' He looked around, and there by his head was a cake of bread baked over hot coals, and a jar of water" (1 Kings 19:5–6). Talk about catering! This was bread from a heavenly bakery.

That's not the only time the angelic kitchens have been busy. For forty years, the angels provided manna for the Israelites as they wandered the desert. Psalm 78:24–25 says that God "rained down manna for the people to eat. . . . Men ate the bread of angels."

It's not impossible for angels to carry out similar missions today. Kenneth Ware was born in my native Tennessee, but after his father's death in World War I, his widowed mother returned to her homeland of Switzerland, and that's where Kenneth grew up. After coming to Christ, he felt called to ministry. He eventually married and sought to minister amid the chaos of World War II. One Saturday morning in September 1944, Kenneth and his wife, Suzie, awoke with nothing to eat and no money for groceries. Suzie decided to tell the Lord what she needed. "Jesus, I need five pounds of potatoes, two pounds of pastry flour, apples, pears, a

Angels even provided physical necessities like food and water for God's people.

cauliflower, carrots, veal cutlets for Saturday, and beef for Sunday." Pausing, she added, "Thank You, Jesus."

At 11:30 that morning, Suzie responded to a rap on the door to find a man with a delivery. He seemed to be in his thirties, with a radiant countenance, tall, light hair, blue eyes, wearing a long blue apron over work clothes. "Mrs. Ware," he said, "I'm bringing you what you asked for."

Going into the kitchen, he emptied the basket onto the table, and Suzie realized the man had brought the items she had prayed for—no more, no less—down to the brand of pastry flour she had wanted. After the man left, the Wares stood by the window to see him leave the building through the only exit, but they never saw him again. He just seemed to vanish.[29]

Sometimes it's not material provisions we need, but inner strength. When the prophet Daniel grew so weak that his strength was gone and he could hardly breathe, an angel touched him and gave him strength (10:17–18). While on a careening ship in the Mediterranean, Paul kept passengers and crew from despair by shouting this testimony over the howling storm:

I urge you to keep up your courage, because not one of you will be lost. . . . Last night an angel of the God whose I am and whom I serve stood beside me and said, "Do not be afraid, Paul. You must stand trial before Caesar; and God has graciously given you the lives of all who sail with you." So keep up your courage, men, for I have faith in God that it will happen just as he told me. (ACTS 27:22–25)

Even Jesus needed the steadying grace of His heavenly Father as conveyed to Him by an angel. Luke 22:43 says that in the Garden of Gethsemane "an angel from heaven appeared to him and strengthened him."

In Isaiah 6, the prophet Isaiah felt unworthy to assume his ministry. "Woe to me!" he cried. "For I am a man of unclean lips" (v. 5). In that moment of misery, God sent a seraph to reassure him of God's forgiving grace.

We can't fathom the ways that angels ferry God's goodness into our daily experiences. Peter used an interesting phrase in one of his letters. He spoke of "God's grace in its various forms" (1 Peter 4:10). The amazing grace of God—His goodness, gifts, blessings, and bounty—come in various forms and are bestowed through manifold means.

God blesses us each day with warming sunshine or replenishing showers, with twittering birds, with harvests of grain that provide our daily bread.

He gives uplifting fellowship, inexhaustible answers to prayer, unfailing providential guidance, and the inner resources for abiding joy, patience, love, and hopefulness. This is the abundant life of John 10:10 and the overflowing cup of Psalm 23:5. It would be surprising, knowing what we know from Scripture, if angels had nothing to do with administering God's grace to His people in their various needs.

Earlier in this chapter I shared Homer Coker's story; let me end it with one from his wife, Joan. She told me about her brother, Carroll Bernard Godwin, who was in the early stages of Alzheimer's. He was scheduled for knee surgery, but the man who took him to the hospital dropped him off at the curb and left. It was the wrong clinic. Mr. Godwin was confused, especially when he found that the clinic was closed.

"My brother had no idea what to do," said Mrs. Coker. "He knew he was supposed to go to UAB Hospital in Birmingham but had no idea how to get there and no means to do so."

A man approached him and asked, "Could I help you?" Mr. Godwin explained his situation as best he could, and the man started walking with him. They walked a long time, when the man said, "Here's a shuttle; let's take this shuttle." They boarded the shuttle, and it took them to the hospital. Once there the man said, "I think you're supposed to go through these doors and up this escalator." Mr. Godwin had no idea where to go, but he followed the man, who took him all the way to the proper office. When Mr. Godwin turned to thank the man, he was gone.[30]

Was it a "good Samaritan" or an angel? We'll know in heaven. But we do know that God's angels frequently mobilize in our direction with bucketfuls of grace. The Bible brims with stories of angels providing crucial help at critical times. They usher God's blessings into our lives at vital moments, heavenly helpers who lend a hand in times of need.

An ancient writer observed that the heavenly host is near but unperceived, just as the stars are in the heaven and the flowers in the field, though a blind man sees them not.[31] For now, it's enough to have the Bible's assurance of their presence and to know . . .

When you're sleeping,

children fair,

Angels keeping watch are there.[32]

SEVEN

Angels

DELIVER US *from* JUDGMENT

*I*t's ironic that talking to people about the wrath of God makes them mad. In most modern pulpits, the message of hell has just about frozen over. Our overly tolerant age is strangely intolerant of anyone warning of the "winepress of the fury of the wrath of God Almighty" (Revelation 19:15). While earlier generations were jolted into revival by warnings of "sinners in the hands of an angry God," our present society rejects the notion of an angry God and resents being labeled sinners.

I want to make a case for fearing God and acknowledging a holy Creator whose essential nature establishes the moral parameters for our universe. God is right in all His ways. Everything in the universe is good to the extent that it reflects His qualities and evil to the extent that it deviates from His nature. The wrath of God is His proper judicial response to the existence of evil and the suffering it inflicts.

What does all this have to do with angels? Much indeed. On many levels, the biblical teaching about angels is interwoven with the truths of divine holiness and holy retribution. In fact, much of the information we have about angels is found in passages relating to God's wrath and judgment.

ANGELS ARE IN AWE OF GOD'S MORAL GOODNESS AND WORSHIP HIM INCESSANTLY FOR HIS PURE AND BURNING HOLINESS.

As we'll see later, they are our worship leaders in heaven, singing, "Holy, Holy, Holy is the LORD Almighty" (Isaiah 6:3). They understand that God's holiness provides the moral baseline for the cosmos and that judgment is the natural consequence of evil. In Revelation 4, the angels around the throne sing a threefold theme, "Holy, Holy, Holy" (v. 8). Four chapters later, an angel hovering over the earth cries another threefold theme, "Woe! Woe! Woe . . . !" (8:13). Just as angels reverence God's holiness, they also pronounce His woe on those rejecting it.

SECOND, ANGELS ARE ACCOUNTABLE TO GOD'S HOLINESS AND ARE THEMSELVES SUBJECT TO JUDGMENT.

Though fallen angels are not the topic of this book, I'd be remiss to neglect them. Scripture clearly and consistently teaches the existence of a diabolical underworld of fallen angels—demons—who followed Lucifer in his rebellion against God. What fathomless layers of judgment and justice have fallen across this invisible sphere of evil! The apostle Peter said bluntly, "God did not spare angels when they sinned, but sent them to hell, putting them into gloomy dungeons to be held for judgment" (2 Peter 2:4). Jude concurs: "The angels who did not keep their positions of authority but abandoned their own home—these he has kept in darkness, bound with everlasting chains for judgment on the great Day" (v. 6).

Jesus said that on the great day of wrath, the Lord will say to those on His left hand, "Depart from me, you who are cursed, into the eternal fire prepared for the devil and his angels" (Matthew 25:41). When Jesus encountered demons during His earthly ministry, they begged Him not to torment them or throw them into the Abyss (Luke 8:31). According to the book of Revelation, the Abyss seems to be a sort of super-maximum security prison in the underworld where the most virulent of the demons are kept until they're unleashed on the earth during the Great Tribulation. Afterward they will be forever consigned to the lake of fire, along with the devil and those who do his bidding (Revelation 9:1–2, 11; 11:7; 17:8; 20:1–2, 10, 15).

THIRD, IN THE BIBLE ANGELS WERE FREQUENTLY THE AGENTS WHO DISPENSED JUDGMENT AND ADMINISTERED THE CHASTISEMENT OF GOD ON SIN-HARDENED INDIVIDUALS AND SOCIETIES.

One of the Bible's earliest episodes with angels had to do with the cities of Sodom and Gomorrah. These towns had become so depraved that there was no goodness left in them. One day two angels arrived in Sodom. They looked like ordinary men, though we can assume they were notably handsome and well built. To put it plainly, the men of Sodom so lusted after these strangers that they wanted to stage a mass orgy and gang rape them. But the angels were on a mission, and the next morning they rained down missiles of divine judgment on the towns and their corrupt inhabitants. God pronounced the sentence, and angels carried out the decree.

In 1 Chronicles 21, we have this stunning passage: "God sent an angel to destroy Jerusalem. But as the angel was doing so, the LORD saw it and was grieved because of the calamity and said to the angel who was destroying the people, 'Enough! Withdraw your hand'" (v. 15).

Much of Revelation describes the waves of catastrophic judgment to be poured on the earth by angels during the Great Tribulation: "I saw in heaven another great and marvelous sign: seven angels with the seven last plagues—last, because with them God's wrath is completed" (15:1).

The apostle Paul wrote of the coming Day of Judgment: "This will happen when the Lord Jesus is revealed from heaven in blazing fire with his powerful angels. He will punish those who do not know God and do not obey the gospel of our Lord Jesus. They will be punished with everlasting destruction and shut out from the presence of the Lord" (2 Thessalonians 1:7–9).

Speaking of that coming Day, Jesus taught, "The harvest is the end of the age, and the harvesters are angels. . . . The angels will come and separate the wicked from the righteous and throw them into the fiery furnace, where there will be weeping and gnashing of teeth" (Matthew 13:39, 49–50).

The angels are God's military police, dispensing justice and keeping our universe from being overwhelmed by the flood of moral evil that threatens. They carry out His decrees, administer His justice, and will inflict His righteous wrath on the world at the end of history.

The angels literally seized Lot's hand and those of his wife and daughters and rushed them to safety before judgment fell.

FOURTH, THE ANGELS DELIVER GOD'S PEOPLE FROM JUDGMENT.

Just as a police officer protects the innocent while punishing the guilty, the angels are responsible for guarding those who are washed in the blood of Calvary. In the story of Sodom, the two-person team came specifically to deliver the one and only righteous family in town. They showed up in the neighborhood of a man named Lot, whom the apostle Peter later described as "a righteous man who was sick of the shameful immorality of the wicked people around him. . . . [He] was tormented in his soul by the wickedness he saw and heard day after day" (2 Peter 2:7–8 NLT).

Lot met the angels, thinking they were simply wayfaring men. Following the rules of ancient hospitality, he offered them a room at his house. "No," they answered, "we will spend the night in the square." But Lot insisted, took them home, and prepared supper for them.

That night the men of the city, young and old, stormed the house to violate the strangers, and only the angelic power of the visitors shielded Lot's family. The next morning, the angels literally seized Lot's hand and those of his wife and daughters and rushed them to safety before judgment fell.

When I think of the story of the angels delivering Lot, I can't help but remember a similar story told me by my friend Dr. Warren Larson, director of the Zwemer Center for Muslim Studies at Columbia International University. In a town near the capital of Islamabad, Pakistan, a wave of persecution threatened the home of a zealous Christian named Qureshi, sometimes called "The Peanut Butter Man" because he makes and markets peanut butter in Pakistan. Local imams tried to force Qureshi to abandon his Christian faith, pressuring him with boycotts and bribes. Failing at that, they incited the Islamic villagers to surround the man's house and burn it to the ground with the Qureshi family inside. As the crowd swarmed the house, Mr. Qureshi gathered his family and tried to prepare them for the end. He reminded them that no suffering could be compared to the glory Christ would reveal. They prayed and sang and waited for the final assault.

Suddenly a voice, clear and sharp, spoke above the roar of the mob: "Do not harm this person and his family. He is a good man. Don't you remember how he helped build a road and repair your canal? Do you forget how he provided water for you when the village well dried up?"

The crowd grew silent. Then one by one people drifted away, until the mob had dispersed. No one ever knew the source of the words. Rumors spread through the town that angels protected the Christians, and Mr. Qureshi was able to continue evangelizing with New Testament boldness.[33]

Has there ever been a time when the Lord's angels delivered you from a situation of impending danger or judgment? It probably happens more often than we realize.

Angels occasionally even save us from ourselves. Scripture's most comical angel story is about Balaam. He wasn't exactly a good man—he was a soothsayer who eventually perished because of his sin. In Numbers 22, he was hired by the king of Moab to curse the children of Israel who were massed at the border. The Lord warned him not to do it, but Balaam decided to travel to the area anyway.

Early the morning of his trip, Balaam saddled his old donkey and the two of them went clopping down the road. An angel of the Lord suddenly appeared, blocking the way. The donkey saw the angel, but Balaam saw nothing. Startled by the sword-wielding angel, the beast bolted into the ditch. Balaam whacked her soundly and yanked her back into the road.

The angel reappeared farther on, this time at a place where the road squeezed between stone walls. The donkey veered against the rocks, smashing Balaam's foot. He angrily struck his donkey again.

The third time it happened, the poor donkey just collapsed under Balaam, sending him toppling to the ground. Mad as fire, Balaam staggered to his feet and struck the animal viciously. That's when one of the oddest miracles of Scripture occurred: "Then the LORD opened the donkey's mouth, and she said to Balaam, 'What have I done to you to make you beat me these three times?'" (v. 28).

Balaam answered the donkey, "You have made a fool of me! If I had a sword in my hand, I would kill you right now." The soothsayer was so livid he didn't realize he was in a shouting match with his donkey—and that the donkey was winning.

"Am I not your own donkey, which you have always ridden, to this day? Have I been in the habit of doing this to you?"

"No," replied Balaam.

At that moment, the Lord opened Balaam's eyes, and he saw the angel standing in the road, sword drawn. Balaam fell on his face. The angel asked, "Why have you beaten your donkey these three times? I have come here to oppose you because your path is a reckless one before me. The donkey saw me and turned away from me these three times. If she had not turned away, I would certainly have killed you by now, but I would have spared her" (vv. 29–32).

I think it's reasonable to assume that angels would much rather shield people from wrath than inflict judgment, and that's one of the reasons they rejoice in heaven whenever a sinner is converted (Luke 15:10).

Perhaps the Lord is somehow blocking your way, warning you that you're on the wrong road. Perhaps you need to find and follow Christ as your Lord and Savior. The book of Romans sums up the gospel like this: "God demonstrates his own love for us in this: While we were still sinners, Christ died for us. Since we have now been justified by his blood, how much more shall we be saved from God's wrath through him!" (5:8–9).

Angels protect us in many other ways, as we'll see in the next pages. But let's end this chapter with an excerpt of one of John Wesley's sermons:

And is it not for the same reason that God is pleased to give His angels charge over us? Namely, that He may endear us and them to each other; that by the increase of our love and gratitude to them, we may find a proportional increase of happiness when we meet in our Father's kingdom. In the meantime, though we may not worship [angels] . . . yet we may "esteem them very highly in love for their works' sake." And we may imitate them in all holiness; suiting our lives to the prayer our Lord himself has taught us; labouring to do his will on earth, as angels do in heaven.[34]

EIGHT

Angels

PROTECT US *in* DANGER

At a speaking engagement in Mississippi, a mutual friend introduced me to Velmarie Burton, who told me her story. Shortly after the birth of her third child, Drew, Velmarie had a visit from her pastor's wife, who delivered a pan of lasagna with a side dish of motherly advice. Pointing her finger at Velmarie, she said very directly: "You need to pray for guardian angels to protect your children from harm."

Velmarie took the counsel seriously and began asking the Lord to station guardian angels to protect the children. Another child came, and Velmarie developed a tradition of taking the children to Destin Beach, Florida, for August vacation. They always stayed in the same condominium on the ground floor. Because of the demands of the family's catfish farm, Velmarie's husband could seldom join them, so her mother or a family friend would go along to help with the children.

In 1993, the group checked into the condo, but this year their room was on the eighth floor. Velmarie slept soundly that Saturday night, but she was aroused from sleep the next morning by frantic banging at the door. She rushed to the door in her pajamas to find a man shouting, "Do you have a baby missing?"

Velmarie stared in horror at the railing of the balcony. Running to the edge, she looked down to see her baby lying motionless on the asphalt eight floors down. She later learned that while she slept, her older boys had awakened and opened the door. The toddlers had wandered onto the walkway and climbed onto a luggage cart. Drew had climbed onto the balcony and toppled over the side.

Velmarie reached the pavement just as sirens filled her ears. The paramedic hovering over the child shouted, "I have a pulse! Give me a backboard and oxygen stat."

The ambulance trip was a blur, but Velmarie will never forget the moment the doctor approached her as she sat alone, still pajama clad, in the waiting room. "Mrs. Burton," he said, "I have no medical explanation for it, but I cannot find anything wrong with your son. I want to do a CAT scan to check for internal injuries, but it appears he's fine."

The next day, newspapers across Florida carried the headlines of the toddler's miracle survival. *USA Today* carried the story, reporting that the child's diaper exploded on impact. One Florida paper ran a headline saying, "Toddler Survives Eight-Floor Tumble." Velmarie believes the headlines should have said: "Angels Protect Toddler During Eight-Story Plunge."

We've already seen how an angelic army protected the prophet Elisha in the city of Dothan, how two angels guarded Lot and his family in Sodom, and how an angel penetrated the security system of a Roman prison to save the apostle Peter.

One of the most famous angelic rescues involved the prophet Daniel, an esteemed statesman in ancient Babylon and Persia. Late in his career, his enemies arranged to have him convicted of a capital crime. Daniel was condemned to a terrible death—being thrown into a pit of hungry lions.

To fear the Lord means to reverence Him and respect His authority.

When the covering was removed the next morning, no one expected to see even a morsel of the old man. But there he was. He had slept soundly, using the lions for both his pillow and blanket. He calmly told the king, "My God sent his angel, and he shut the mouths of the lions. They have not hurt me, because I was found innocent in his sight" (Daniel 6:22).

Is Daniel's angel still on duty? Two blockbuster verses in the Bible reassure us that the same angels are watching over us today. Both are in Psalms, in the heart of the Bible, and they are verses we can claim as promises for ourselves.

PSALM 34:7. David composed this Psalm after a terrifying experience. Pursued by the armies of King Saul, David had fled across the border into enemy territory only to be trapped by the king of Gath. His only hope was to bluff his way out of danger, which he did by feigning insanity. Later, in Psalm 34, he credited his escape to answered prayer and angelic aid. "I sought the Lord, and he answered me," he wrote. "This poor man called, and the Lord heard him; he saved him out of all his troubles. The angel of the LORD encamps around those who fear him, and he delivers them" (vv. 4, 6–7).

No angel showed up visibly, yet David believed his escape was facilitated by unseen angelic assistance as he feared the Lord. To fear the Lord means to reverence Him and respect His authority.

Psalm 34 is full of exhortations to fear and obey the Lord. Verse 9 says, "Fear the LORD, you his saints, for those who fear him lack nothing." The next verses tell us that fearing the Lord results in keeping our tongues from evil and our lips from lying. It results in turning from what is wrong, instead doing good and seeking peace. In the process, we have the fabulous promise of verse 7: "The angel of the LORD encamps around those who fear him, and he delivers them."

PSALM 91:11. "For he will command his angels concerning you to guard you in all your ways." A good way to remember this reference is to think of it as your 911 verse, with an added 1 because it works so well in extreme emergencies—9111, or Psalm 91:11.

In my book *Real Stories for the Soul*, I wrote about Charles Herbert Lightoller, a respected seaman for the White Star Line who was assigned to the maiden voyage of the *Titanic*. He was just drifting off to sleep on April 14, 1912, when he felt a bump in the ship's motion. Hopping from his bunk, he learned that the *Titanic* had struck an iceberg. As the horrors of that night unfolded, Lightoller found himself standing on the roof of the officers' quarters, helping women and children into lifeboats. He later said he would never forget the sight of the greenish water creeping up the steps toward his feet. Finally there was nothing left to do but walk, as it were, into the freezing waters of the North Atlantic.

The shock of the frigid water stunned him, and as he struggled to swim away from the ship, he was suddenly drawn back and pinned against a ventilation grate at the base of a funnel that went all the way down to boiler room six. As he was pulled under water, a Scripture came clearly to his mind—Psalm 91:11: "He will command his angels concerning you to guard you in all your ways."

At that moment, a blast of hot air exploded from the belly of the ship, shooting Lightoller like a missile to the surface of the ocean. He managed to grab a piece of wood but went down a second time. This time he resurfaced beside an overturned lifeboat and managed to pull himself on to it. Turning, he watched the last moments of the *Titanic*. Her stern swung up in the air until the ship was in "an absolutely perpendicular position." Then she slowly sank down into the water, with only a small gulp as her stern disappeared beneath the waves. About thirty men were atop the lifeboat, and together they recited the Lord's Prayer; then Lightoller took command of the boat and guided them to safety.[35]

How often has an angel kept our heads above water when our ship was going down? Psalm 91:11 is such a powerful verse on angelology that you may want to take time right now to read the entire Psalm.

Of course, there are times when we *do* suffer harm. We know by reading the rest of the Bible that God doesn't roll us in bubble wrap and pamper us all the way to heaven. The heroes of the Bible suffered, and some were slain for their faith. God's angels don't always deliver us in the way we'd choose, but always in the best way. We can take promises such as Psalm 91:11 literally, but we must leave the methods and means of their fulfillment to the Lord and His angelic servants. When we're in their care, how temporary our hurts! How permanent our blessings! The sufferings of this present life aren't worth comparing with the glory to be revealed. Our light and momentary afflictions are achieving for us an eternal weight of glory. Along the way, we have more protection from our angelic friends than we know.

Perhaps this is a good time to bring up the subject of guardian angels. As I recorded the story of Velmarie Burton's toddler, who plunged eight stories to the asphalt below, I thought of what Jesus said about children in Matthew 18:10: "See that you do not look down on one of these little ones. For I tell you that their angels in heaven always see the face of My Father in heaven."

Does this imply that every child has a guardian angel? Every person? Every church? The seven letters in Revelation 2 and 3 were each addressed to the "angel" overseeing these seven congregations. Since the word *angel* means "messenger," some commentators believe the letters were addressed to the human messengers—the pastors—of each church. But other commentaries point out that numerous other occurrences of the word *angel* in the book of Revelation refer to literal angels.

God's angels don't always deliver us in the way we'd choose

So are angels assigned to individual congregations? Do we have our own guardian angels? The early Christians seemed to think so. When Peter was delivered from prison in Acts 12, he went to a secret location where the Christians were praying for him. When he knocked at the door, the housekeeper was so excited that she ran to tell everyone without letting him in. Peter's friends couldn't believe he was free. "You're out of your mind," they told her. . . . "It must be his angel" (v. 15).

My opinion is that these passages are interesting, but I'm not willing to base an entire doctrine of guardian angels on them. They just don't give enough information. We do know from the Bible that angels come and go. I believe they rotate on assignment. We have a host of angels watching over us. One of them very well may be in charge of us as our "guardian angel," and if so, I'm eager to meet mine in heaven. But I don't believe he does all the work alone. As John Wesley said:

A convoy attends,

A ministering host of invisible friends.

Reverend Edward King entered the ministry in 1854, in the English village of Wheatley. One night he was called to visit a dying man a mile or two away. The night was dark, but King trudged on by foot, only to arrive at the home and discover that no one was sick after all. He returned home perplexed.

Years later, when he was bishop of Lincoln, King made another visit, this time to a condemned prisoner under sentence of death. The criminal asked King if he remembered his useless nocturnal walk of years ago. "It was I who gave you the false message," said the man, "to lure you out that I might rob you." The bishop, curious, asked the man why he hadn't carried out his plan.

"I lay in hiding," said the man, "but when you came near, I saw you were not alone."

"But I was alone," said the bishop.

"No, you were not. There was a mysterious looking stranger walking close behind you, and he followed you to your home and then disappeared. My chance was gone, and I experienced a sensation I never felt before."[36]

As John Newton, author of "Amazing Grace," wrote in his hymn "The Believer's Safety," based on Psalm 91:

Angels

UNSEEN ATTEND THE SAINTS,

And bear them in their arms,

TO CHEER THE SPIRIT WHEN IT FAINTS,

And guard the life from harms.

NINE

Angels

ASSIST GOD
in ANSWERING
OUR PRAYERS

When I told my friend John Hooper that I was working on this book, he said he might have a story for me. John's story was so personal that he had never shared it with anyone except his wife, Crystal.

When John was eight years old, his father came home drunk. This happened frequently, and it always filled the children with dread because their dad could fly into a rage in an instant. The man's tirades usually involved the four children as a unit, which at least allowed the youngsters to stick together during the ensuing chaos. But on this particular night, John was singled out. As the family tensely gathered for dinner, John said something innocuous that sent his dad into a rampage. The man ordered John to his room, adding ominously, "I will meet you there!"

The boy bolted from the table and ran up the stairs to his room. Closing the door, he knelt by his bed and tried to pray. His Gideon New Testament was on the night table, but John's hands were shaking too hard to read it. His eyes filled with tears. "Jesus," he stammered, "I think I'm going to die tonight. So I'm asking You for one of two things please. Would you either protect me here on earth tonight, or would You take me up to heaven to be with You? Either way, I know I'll be safe."

At that moment, John heard a commotion downstairs. A stranger had showed up in the kitchen. It was an oven repairman making a late and unexpected call. The stranger's presence distracted John's dad, defused the family crisis, and short-circuited the booze-induced rage. A few minutes later, John's mother called him to come back downstairs and finish his supper. As he entered the kitchen, John saw a man with a warm smile. The stranger looked purposefully at John, winked, and went about his task.

"I've always felt he was an angel in work clothes," John told me, "an angel who came in the form of an oven repairman."[37]

Hebrews 4:16 also tells us to "approach the throne of grace with confidence, so that we may receive mercy and find grace to help us in our time of need." Seven times in His Upper Room Discourse in John 13–17, Jesus said that if we ask anything in His name, He will do it. The apostle John later restated the promise like this: "This is the confidence we have in approaching God: that if we ask anything according to his will, he hears us. And if we know that he hears us—whatever we ask—we know that we have what we asked of him" (1 John 5:14–15).

Whether the Lord allows angels to eavesdrop on our prayers, I don't know. I do believe He frequently employs them in answering prayer: case in point, the prophet Daniel. As prime minister of Babylon and Persia, Daniel had a lifelong habit of retiring to his private quarters three times a day to spend time talking to the Lord (Daniel 6:10). On one occasion, Daniel had been poring over the writings of the prophet Jeremiah. He came to understand from Jeremiah's prophecies that the time had come for Israel to return from exile and once again repopulate the Promised Land. Daniel made this a matter of earnest prayer. One afternoon, the angel Gabriel showed up during his prayer time. "As soon as you began to pray," Gabriel told him, "an answer was given, which I have come to tell you" (Daniel 9:23). Daniel made the request, God bestowed the grace, and an angel brought the answer.

In the next chapter, we have an even more remarkable story. Daniel was given a graphic vision by direct revelation from God. Deeply troubled, Daniel prayed earnestly to understand the vision. Three weeks passed. One day Daniel accompanied some men who were inspecting the banks of the Tigris River. Looking up, he saw a man dressed in linen with a belt of gold around his waist. His body was like topaz, his face like lightning, his eyes on fire. His arms and legs resembled burnished bronze that flashed in the sunshine. His voice was like the roar of a stadium.

The sudden appearance of this spectacular stranger drained the strength from Daniel's body like air from a balloon, and he collapsed. At once an angel stood beside him, touched him, and helped him to his hands and knees and gradually to his feet. The next words we read fill us with wonder. The angel said:

> Don't be afraid, Daniel. Since the first day you began to pray for understanding and to humble yourself before your God, your request has been heard in heaven. I have come in answer to your prayer. But for twenty-one days the spirit prince of the kingdom of Persia blocked my way. Then Michael, one of the archangels, came to help me, and I left him there with the spirit prince of the kingdom of Persia. Now I am here to explain what will happen to your people in the future. (10:12–14 NLT)

There's an invisible grid around our planet where unseen forces deploy.

No further explanation is given, but taken at face value, it appears that at the moment Daniel began praying, the answer was issued without delay, just as in the previous chapter. But powerful demonic forces had blocked the pathway of the angel bearing the answer. The impasse lasted a full three weeks until the archangel Michael arrived on the scene with his superior authority. The standoff was ended, and the delayed angel sped on to Daniel with the answer to his prayer.

I'm staggered to know that there is so much invisible static in the unseen spheres. It's remarkable to think that our prayers to God and His answers to us may pass through the territory of the "prince of the power of the air" (Ephesians 2:2 NKJV). It's sobering to know that angels bearing the answers to our prayers are opposed and sometimes delayed by what Paul called "the rulers . . . the authorities . . . the spiritual forces of evil in the heavenly realms" (6:12). There's an invisible grid around our planet where unseen forces deploy. How thankful we should be for every answer to prayer that comes to us from day to day.

Nowhere does the Bible suggest we're to pray to angels. Paul warned the Colossians not to be deceived by anyone veering off into the worship of angels (2:18). Even though some of the biblical characters spoke to angels, there's no indication in Scripture that we're to offer prayers to them. But they do seem to play a role in the process of prayer, especially as they assist God in the delivery of His answers to our earnest petitions.

Terry Hammack, who lived next door to me in college, has worked for the Lord in Nigeria for many years. Some time ago, when he and Sue were stateside, they told me about the riots that broke out in the northern city of Kano in October of 1991. The trouble had started when a German evangelist announced a series of open-air evangelistic meetings in the area. This triggered a violent reaction by the Muslim population. Christian businesses and churches were targeted for looting and destruction, and believers found themselves in grave danger. Terry was able to evacuate his family to safety, but since he operated the communications equipment, he felt he should stay alongside the national leader, Pastor Garba.

On Tuesday morning, thousands of rioters surrounded the mission, wanting to burn it and the hospital to the ground. Pastor Garba met the crowd at the gate in a flowing traditional gown. He tried to reason with the mob, but the eyes of many seemed focused on an open space in the courtyard behind him, as though they saw something that startled them.

The mob moved down the street, but rumors began flying around town that the mission was on fire. One Muslim leader, who had paid a deposit for his wife to give birth at the mission hospital, showed up to see if he had lost his money. He reported fires burning on top of the walls and buildings, which prevented him from entering. But the fires didn't appear to be normal, and the buildings weren't consumed. He went home and called other religious men to view the phenomenon. They all saw the fires, which burned all day Tuesday, Wednesday, and Thursday.

Throughout those days, Terry and his compatriots, trapped inside the walls, expected an attack, but none came. "Though Pastor Garba and I engaged in prayer walks of protection around the walls during those days," he said, "we ourselves did not see the fires. But later, our coworker Janet Schneidermann, hearing the story, reminded us of Zechariah 2:5: "'And I myself will be a wall of fire around it,' declares the LORD, 'and I will be its glory within.'"[38]

There's more activity in the heavenly realms than we realize, and angels have more to do with answering our prayers than we know. As Martin Luther once quipped, the angels have long arms. They stand in the presence of God, yet reach you and me in our times of need.

TEN

Angels

TEACH US
to WORSHIP

The incessant ringing of the phone awakened David and Denise Love of Edinburg, Texas, at 3 a.m. The news was bad. David's brother, Mike, a police officer, had been killed. David, distraught beyond words, headed toward the bathroom to shower and dress while Denise hurriedly packed for the trip. When David emerged from the shower, he seemed much calmer. He asked Denise to sing the hymn "Be Still, My Soul." Denise found a hymnbook and sang it to him as he finished packing. On the way to the airport, he asked her to sing it again. As they waited for the airplane, he asked her to sing it a third time. His countenance was one of peace.

On the anniversary of Mike's death a year later, David and Denise reminisced about that tragic night. Denise asked, "Why did you keep asking me to sing that song?"

"Didn't I tell you?" he replied. "When I got in the shower, the ceiling suddenly parted and the angels in heaven sang that hymn to me. It gave me the strength I needed to make it through the next painful days."[39]

Some writers have questioned whether angels actually sing, and this is a valid discussion. But I cannot imagine tuneless angels. God loves music. He filled the Bible with hymns. He filled the universe with singing creatures—from songbirds to giant blue whales. He puts songs in our mouths and melodies in our hearts. Can we really believe there's no music around the throne, that angels are somehow excluded from God's singing creation?

It's true that the verbs used for angelic communication are usually words like *said* and *called*, but those words don't exclude the medium of song. Who can imagine the night skies over Bethlehem filled with a host of choiring angels who weren't able to sing? Revelation is packed with hymns, so it's reasonable to assume they were sung. Does anyone really think their praise is rendered in a monotone?

Revelation 5:8–11 tells us that the twenty-four elders (who perhaps represent the raptured church) and the four living creatures (who seem to be cherubim-like angelic creatures) all had harps, "and they sang a new song" to the Lamb (v. 9). Verses 11–12 say, "Then I looked and heard the voice of many angels, numbering thousands upon thousands, and ten thousand times ten thousand. They encircled the throne and the living creatures and the elders. In a loud voice they sang: 'Worthy is the Lamb.'" Verse 13 goes on to say: "Then I heard every creature in heaven and on earth and under the earth and on the sea, and all that is in them, singing."[40]

Psalm 148:2 declares, "Praise him, all his angels, praise him, all his heavenly hosts." According to Hebrews 12:22, the presence of God is surrounded by "thousands upon thousands of angels in joyful assembly."

British hymnist Reginald Heber composed one of the greatest anthems of Christendom: "Holy, Holy, Holy." The second verse refers to two distinct categories of worshiping angels:

Cherubim and seraphim
falling down before Thee,
who was, and is, and evermore shall be.

WHO ARE SERAPHIM?

This rank or species of angels is mentioned only once in Scripture, when the prophet Isaiah was ordained to the ministry. In chapter 6, Isaiah testified:

> I saw the Lord seated on a throne, high and exalted, and the train of his robe filled the temple. Above him were seraphs, each with six wings: With two wings they covered their faces, with two they covered their feet, and with two they were flying. And they were calling to one another: "Holy, holy, holy is the LORD Almighty; the whole earth is full of his glory." At the sound of their voices the doorposts and thresholds shook and the temple was filled with smoke.
>
> "Woe to me!" I cried. "I am ruined! For I am a man of unclean lips". . . .
>
> Then one of the seraphs flew to me with a live coal in his hand, which he had taken with tongs from the altar. With it he touched my mouth and said, "See, this has touched your lips; your guilt is taken away and your sin is atoned for."
>
> Then I heard the voice of the Lord saying, "Whom shall I send? And who will go for us?" And I said, "Here am I. Send me!" (vv. 1–8).

Seraphs and *seraphim* probably come from an ancient Hebrew verb meaning "to burn." If so, we could describe seraphim as "burning ones" or "fiery ones." These six-winged creatures are both awesome and awestruck, both holy and humble, able to fly and capable of speaking. Their praise shook the temple to its foundations. They conveyed to Isaiah an assurance of God's grace and buttressed him as he surrendered himself fully to the ministry to which God was calling him.

WHO ARE THE CHERUBIM?

Whereas seraphim are mentioned only once in the Bible, cherubim are mentioned eighty-nine times. The first angels we encounter in the Bible are cherubim, whose flashing swords guarded the way to the tree of life (Genesis 3:24).

Several years ago, I delved into what the Bible says about the Old Testament tabernacle, the elaborate tent Moses constructed as a worship center in the wilderness. Incredibly, the Bible devotes fifty chapters to the tabernacle, and its every aspect points prophetically

These six-winged creatures are both awesome and awestruck . . . their praise shook the temple to its foundations.

toward Christ Jesus. One of the things that surprised me was the preponderance of cherubim. Images of this strange variety of angel were everywhere. They showed up in carvings, statues, engravings, and embroideries, including the two great cherubim that loomed over the ark of the covenant in the Most Holy Place.

Isaiah 37:16 describes God as the "Lord Almighty . . . enthroned between the cherubim."

When Solomon built the temple as a permanent replacement for the well-worn tabernacle, he followed the same plan. Cherubim were all over the place. "In the inner sanctuary he made a pair of cherubim of olive wood. . . . On the walls all around the temple . . . he carved cherubim. . . . On the two olive wood doors he carved cherubim. . . . He also made two pine doors. . . . He carved cherubim . . . on them" (1 Kings 6:23, 29, 32, 34–35).

Why so many cherubim in the tabernacle and the temple? I'll propose two reasons: First, the Holy Place in the temple was filled with images of angels because it was the localized, earthly representation of the true and eternal throne of God in heaven, which is surrounded by angels. Second, the presence of these cherubim reminded the priests and worshipers that as they approached the throne of almighty God, they were at that moment in the presence of an invisible multitude of holy angels, hovering around them.

Can you imagine being Israel's high priest, entering this cube-shaped chamber once a year—the Holy of Holies? Positioned at the far end of the room sat a gilded chest known as the ark of the covenant, and over it towered two golden cherubim, their wings flying upward. It would visually remind you that you had just entered the ethereal presence of Almighty God and that you were surrounded on every side by actual cherubim—and who knows how many!

That's worship! Whenever we approach the throne of grace, we're coming into the presence of Him who is thrice Holy, and we're joining the heavenly hosts hovering near. Together—you and me, the cherubim and seraphim and all the angels, the seen and the unseen—we join in praising Him who was and is and evermore shall be. That's what happens as we worship, both privately and with others.

The Bible says, "Since we have confidence to enter the Most Holy Place by the blood of Jesus, by a new and living way opened for us through the curtain, that is, his body, and since we have a great priest over the house of God, let us draw near to God with a sincere heart in full assurance of faith" (Hebrews 10:19–22).

The prophet Ezekiel, a young priest consigned to a refugee camp in Babylon, was given glimpses of actual cherubim. God wanted to encourage him. Since Ezekiel was unable to work in the temple with the symbolic depictions of cherubim, his eyes were opened to see the real thing. He saw the throne of God appearing in a whirlwind, conveyed on a sort of movable platform, accompanied by actual cherubim. Ezekiel describes them as humanlike in form, but with four faces and four wings.[41]

When we come to the book of Revelation, we meet a set of angelic creatures who closely resemble Ezekiel's cherubim. The apostle John, writing in Revelation 4, said:

In the center, around the throne, were four living creatures, and they were covered with eyes, in front and in back. The first living creature was like a lion, the second was like an ox, the third had a face like a man, the fourth was like a flying eagle. Each of the four living creatures had six wings and was covered with eyes all around, even under his wings. Day and night they never stop saying: "Holy, holy, holy is the Lord God Almighty, who was, and is, and is to come." (vv. 6–8)

Verses 9–11 go on to say:

> Whenever the living creatures give glory, honor and thanks to him who sits on the throne and who lives for ever and ever, the twenty-four elders fall down before him who sits on the throne, and worship him who lives for ever and ever. They lay their crowns before the throne and say: "You are worthy, our Lord and God, to receive glory and honor and power; for you created all things, and by your will they were created and have their being."

If, as some expositors believe, the church has been raptured at this point in the book of Revelation, the twenty-four elders may represent the church of all the ages. If so, Revelation 4 offers a resplendent picture of angels leading Christians in thunderous worship around the throne in the New Jerusalem as the world below braces for the Great Tribulation to be unleashed in Revelation 6–18.

In Revelation 19, as Christ prepares to come to earth again at the moment of the Second Coming, all of heaven erupts in worship, led by the angels: "Hallelujah! For our Lord God Almighty reigns. Let us rejoice and be glad and give Him glory!" (vv. 6–7)

How much we could learn about worship if, as we read through the Bible, we noticed how God's seraphim and cherubim worship Him, along with all the heavenly hosts! Perhaps this chapter will whet our appetites. I don't know about you, but I'm not a gifted singer. I can't seem to hit the right tones or sustain a clear note. My mind wanders during songs at church. My spirit sometimes sags even while listening to rousing Christian music or beautifully spoken prayers. Some days I crawl into bed feeling that I've not been a very active worshiper that day.

But it helps to imagine the ceiling parting enough to reveal—by faith— an echo of praise from around the throne. We can picture cherubim and seraphim falling down before God. We can see His angelic choirs hovering around the enthroned Trinity, sometimes soaring through the skies, sometimes falling on their faces, sometimes directing the music, some- times singing alongside our loved ones who have gone on before, sometimes punctuating their praise with outbursts of "Hallelujah!"

When we praise the Lord, we're simply tuning in to the great worship service constantly occurring in the highest heaven, led by these mysterious multitudes. What majesty!

All hail the power of Jesus' name!

LET ANGELS PROSTRATE FALL;

Bring forth the royal diadem,

AND CROWN HIM LORD OF ALL.

ELEVEN

Angels

USHER US *to* HEAVEN

*M*rs. Agnes Frazier was the oldest member of our church and a woman of deep piety and enthusiastic spirituality. At age ninety-five, her health failed, and I received a call.

"Mrs. Agnes is asking for you," her nurse said. When I entered her room, she was almost too weak to look up at me. Her words were indistinct at times, but it soon became clear that she wanted to see me because she was curious about "these men."

"What men?" I asked.

"I keep seeing these two men."

"What do they look like?"

"Two men, dressed in white from head to foot, are standing at the end of my bed. I don't know what to tell them. What should I say if they ask me something?"

"Tell them," I said at length, "that you belong to Jesus."

That seemed to satisfy her. "Yes," she said, "I'll tell them I belong to Jesus." Shortly after, she fell asleep in Christ, and those two angels, I believe, ushered her to heaven.

In 2 Kings 2, the prophet Elijah came to the end of his earthly duties, and God decided to call him home to heaven. As he and his disciple, Elisha, were walking along in a remote area, their conversation was cut short. Suddenly "a chariot of fire and horses of fire appeared and separated the two of them, and Elijah went up to heaven in a whirlwind. Elisha saw this and cried out, 'My father! My father! The chariots and horsemen of Israel!' And Elisha saw him no more" (vv. 11–12).

It's true that Elijah didn't die, but it's equally true that the angels ushered him to heaven in dramatic fashion. That seems to be part of their job description—to escort us from this world to the next at the end of our earthly tour of duty.

This will certainly happen at the end of the age when the Lord Jesus returns for His people. He'll snatch us to heaven, and the angels will assist as escorts and ushers. Speaking about His return, Jesus said, "He will send his angels with a loud trumpet call, and they will gather his elect from the four winds, from one end of the heavens to the other" (Matthew 24:31).

In Revelation 21 and 22, an angel gave the apostle John a tour of the New Jerusalem. He showed him the city from a distance, then up close; then he accompanied him through the gates, down the golden street, and to the very center of the city with its crystal river, broad park, and glorious throne. If an angel served as the tour guide for John, it seems sensible that angels will be our orientation guides when we, too, arrive in the celestial city.

One of the most reassuring words on this subject comes from the lips of our Lord Jesus. In Luke 16, He told the story of a beggar named Lazarus who suffered from a loathsome skin disease and from abject poverty. This poor man ate from the garbage while dogs licked his sores. But Jesus said, "The time came when the beggar died and the angels carried him to Abraham's side" (v. 22).

Notice that *angels* is plural. Commentator Matthew Henry suggested that one angel could surely have done the job, but the Lord sent an entire convoy, for saints should be escorted home not only in safety but also with honor.

The Greek word used here for *carry* can mean to lead, take away, carry, or transfer. It implies a sufficient means of transport from one place to another.

The phrase "Abraham's side" is meant to show us that this man, Lazarus, who was a wretched beggar on earth, soon found himself walking around with Abraham, Isaac, Jacob, and all the great heroes of God who had arrived in heaven before him. It suggests literal, conscious fellowship with our friends in paradise. In Matthew 8:11, Jesus used similar language in speaking of the joy of going to be with Abraham, Isaac, and Jacob.

Luke 16:22 signifies a precious promise for all of us who occasionally worry about the moment of death. It reassures us we have nothing to fear, for Christ has paved the way and the angels will see to it that we don't make the trip alone.

Laura Whiteaker, a member of my church in Nashville, told me about her eighty-eight-year-old grandmother, universally known as Grandma, who had suffered a severe stroke. One Friday evening in late June 2004, Laura's mother, Carol, went by the nursing home to check on Grandma. Walking into the room, Carol saw at once that all was not well. She leaned over the bed and said, "Grandma, this is Carol. How are you today?"

"Carol," the woman replied with effort. "You are so good to me and I love you so much. I feel so bad today, but there are angels all around me and they are taking such good care of me." Though her words came with difficulty, Grandma noticeably emphasized that last phrase: . . . *such good care of me.*

"On the following Monday night, Grandma went home to be with the God she had served since she was a little girl," Carol told me. "I believe as surely as I know my name that those same angels she saw in the room on Friday night stayed on Monday night. She is now with Him forever!"

CHRIST HAS PAVED THE WAY,

and the angels will see to it

THAT WE DON'T MAKE THE TRIP ALONE.

Perhaps the best perspective on this I've ever read is found in a letter written on March 3, 1877, by the Reverend John S. C. Abbot, a Congregational pastor in New England. Knowing he was dying, Abbot picked up his pen to scribble this final note to a friend, J. Dewitt Miller:

I am pillowed upon a sick and dying bed, with a little tablet in my hands. I can, without much difficulty, pencil lines to my friends. I suffer very little pain. My mind, it seems to me, was never more clear and joyous. The physicians assure me that I am liable at any moment to die. I am happy. I do not see how anyone can be more happy out of heaven. . . . I am expecting every hour that a group of loving angels will come and say to me: "Brother, God has sent us to convey you to heaven—the chariot is waiting."

All the infirmities of the flesh and sin will vanish from body and soul. I shall be the congenial companion of angels in that most wonderful of all conceivable journeys from earth to heaven. . . .

When the angelic summons comes, I shall be an "heir of God." . . . The escort will be glorious; angels loving me with a brother's love, and God will have made me worthy of their love. . . .

Angels and archangels, cherubim and seraphim, will gather around us with their congratulations. We shall see God, His throne, the splendor of His court, understand all the mysteries of His being, and enter upon blessings inconceivable, forever and ever!

All this I believe, my dear friend, as fully as I believe in my own existence. And I may enter upon this enjoyment before night shall darken around me.

Yours, affectionately, John S. C. Abbott.[42]

Are not all angels sent to serve those who will inherit salvation? Our angel friends transport blessings to our lives, deliver us from judgment, protect us from danger, guide us through life, assist God in answering our prayers, teach us to worship, and usher us to heaven. And that's merely the beginning! Just think of the fun we're going to have with them in eternity!

I shall be the congenial companion of angels in that most wonderful of all conceivable journeys from earth to heaven.

Are not all angels

sent to serve those *who will inherit salvation?*

CONCLUSION

MY LORD!

The Lord Jesus spoke frequently about angels, but perhaps His soberest words are found in Luke 12:8–9: "I tell you, whoever acknowledges me before men, the Son of Man will also acknowledge him before the angels of God. But he who disowns me before men will be disowned before the angels of God."

He was telling us that there is a God, an eternity, a heaven and hell, powerful contingents of both angels and demons, and a day of eternal reckoning.

Angels, according to Hebrews 1:14, are sent to serve those who inherit salvation. Salvation is what Christ Jesus came to provide. It's the Lord Jesus Christ Himself, not angels, who can forgive our sins and give us eternal life. He is God "now in flesh appearing," the Savior who lived a righteous life, died on Calvary's cross, and rose from a Judean tomb—all for us. "Salvation is found in no one else," says Acts 4:12, "for there is no other name under heaven given to men by which we must be saved."

Our part is simple. The Bible says, "If you confess with your mouth, 'Jesus is Lord,' and believe in your heart that God raised him from the dead, you will be saved" (Romans 10:9).

You can do that now by simply and sincerely asking Him as best you know how to forgive your sins, be your Savior, and become the Lord of your life. You can bow your head and do that just as you are right now. Then follow it up by developing the habit of reading your Bible every day, learning to pray, attending a good church each week, and looking for ways to share your newfound faith with others.

Trusting Christ

as your Savior

is a decision that makes

the angels sing!

NOTES

1. Richard Hendrix in an interview with the author. Used with permission.

2. Based on a personal conversation with Dr. Richard S. Hipps. Used with permission.

3. Quoted by Alfred Fowler in *Our Angel Friends in Ministry and Song* (Alfred Fowler, 1903), 374.

4. From Spurgeon's sermon "God's Providence," published on October 15, 1908.

5. David Jeremiah, *What the Bible Says about Angels* (Sisters, OR: Multnomah Books, 1996), 22.

6. The Pentateuch is the name given to the first five books of the Bible.

7. Taken largely verbatim from a personal letter to the author from Terence Hammack, dated August 15, 2010.

8. Quoted in *The Female Poets of America*, by Rufus Wilmot Griswold (New York: James Miller Publishers, 1873), 361.

9. *The Table Talk of Martin Luther*, translated by William Hazlitt (London: George Bell and Sons, 1902), 246.

10. Quoted in *Our Angel Friends in Ministry and Song*, 5.

11. Charles Hodge, *Systematic Theology, Vol. 1* (NY: Scribner Armstrong & Co, 1873), 638.

12. *The Familiar Discourses of Dr. Martin Luther*, translated by Captain Henry Bell (London: Baldwin, Craddock, and Joy, 1818), 316.

13. John Wesley, *Sermons on Several Occasions, Vol. 2* (New York: Carlton & Phillips, 1855), 134.

14. Quoted in *Our Angel Friends in Ministry and Song*, 46.

15. Albert Barnes, *Notes Explanatory and Practical on the Epistle to the Hebrews* (London: Knight and Son, 1855), 66.

16. Based on my conversations and subsequent e-mail from Dr. Mary Ruth Wisehart. Used with permission.

17. Wesley, *Sermons on Several Occasions, Vol. 2*, 137.

18. Merle Inniger, written by his wife, Gloria, as Merle passed away in 2006, and passed on to me by our mutual friend Warren Larson, director of the Zwemer Center for Muslim Studies at Columbia International University. The Innigers were missionaries to Pakistan. Used with permission.

19. From Martin Luther's hymn "A Mighty Fortress Is Our God," written in 1529 and translated from German by Frederic H. Hedge in 1853.

20. Based on e-mail correspondence with Sharnel Smith in August of 2010. Used with permission.

21. Quoted in *Our Angel Friends in Ministry and Song* (Alfred Fowler, 1903), 57.

22. Norman Macleod, *Parish Papers* (NY: Robert Carter and Brothers, 1863), 123.

23. Quoted in *Our Angel Friends in Ministry and Song*, 60.

24. Catherine Marshall, *A Man Called Peter* (Grand Rapids, MI: Chosen Books, 1951), 28–29.

25. It's also possible that the star followed by the Magi was actually an angel who was leading them to the Christ child.

26. *The Ecclesiastical History of Socrates* (London: George Bell & Sons, 1892), 197; and *The Greek Ecclesiastical Historians* (London: Samuel Bagster and Sons, 1894), book III, 184.

27. Based on an e-mail interview with help from Paul and Gloria Willoughby, October 2010. Used with permission.

28. Personal interview with the author. Used by permission.

29. Taken from a tract entitled "Introducing Rev. Kenneth Ware of Paris, France," a transcript of a broadcast sermon on the ABC Network by C. M. Ward on April 19, 1959. Used by permission of Assemblies of God World Missions, with special thanks to Gloria Robinett, archivist.

30. Personal interview with the author. Used by permission.

31. F. N. Peloubet, "October 30, Elisha at Dothan, 2 Kings 6:8–23," *Select Notes on the International Sunday School Lessons* (Boston, MA: American Baptist Publication Society, 1903), 301.

32. Matthias Barr, nineteenth-century Scottish poet, in *The Children's Service Book for Church and Home*, edited by Rev. H. Martyn Hart (London: Daldy, Isbister, & Co, 1875), 105.

33. Told to me by Dr. Warren Larson. Used with permission. You can read more about Mr. Qureshi in *The Peanut Butter Man* by R. W. Irwin, a missionary with the Evangelical Alliance Mission in Pakistan from 1956 to 1995. It's published by Tate Publishing & Enterprises, 2010.

34. Wesley, *Sermons on Several Occasions, Vol. 2*, 166.

35. Robert J. Morga n, *Real Stories for the Soul* (Nashville: Thomas Nelson, 2000), 249–251. Pieced together from several books and Internet articles

about the Titanic. Lightoller's story also appeared in the Congressional Record of the investigation of the sinking of the Titanic. Lightoller lived until December 8, 1952. Interestingly, he was an adherent of the Christian Science faith.

36. Alida Stanwood, *Reinforcements* (New York: R. R. Beam & Co., 1915), 148.

37. Told to me in person and e-mail from John Hooper of Nashville, Tennessee. Used with permission.

38. Based on conversations and subsequent e-mails from Terry and Sue Hammack of SIM. Used with permission.

39. Based on e-mail correspondence with David and Denise Love. Used with permission.

40. The verb in verse 9 is clearly a word for "sing." The verb in verses 12 and 13 is *lego*, which means to "talk" or "communicate." It can mean either "speak" or "sing," and since it's often used before portions in Revelation that are obviously poetical hymns, the NIV translators chose to use the word "sing."

41. You can read his vivid descriptions in Ezekiel 1, 9, 10, 11, 28, and 41.

42. Quoted by S. B. Shaw in *Touching Incidents and Remarkable Answers to Prayer* (Lansing, MI: J. W. Hazelton, 1893), 141–143.